PRAISE

SEEKING JOY THROUGH THE GOSPEL OF LUKE
BY CHRISTINE TRIMPE

Christine Trimpe wants to see everyone live life kicked up a notch. She is like a stampede of encouragement gone full throttle! God has given her an undeniable thirst for refreshing everyone who crosses her path. *Seeking Joy* takes us from the Christmas chaos in a weary world to the true meaning of Christmas and the gift of everlasting joy. I love how she brings the people of the Bible to the forefront and focuses on how we can relate with them even in today's world. She is truly AH-mazing!

—Tammy Whitehurst, *Joy for the Journey*
Motivational Speaker and co-owner of the Christian Communicators
Conference

The word *joy* brought Christine and I together because we are both seekers of "His" joy. As I read through her *Seeking Joy through the Gospel of Luke* Advent devotional, I discovered she was taking me on a journey of finding "His" great joy. I love Christmas and celebrating our Savior's birth. The devotional begins on December 1, in Luke 1, and Christine shares a familiar story with fresh insight from her journey of seeking "His" joy. Every day in December you read another chapter and dive deeper into her joy-seeking adventure. The next thing I knew, the journey was mine too. By the time you reach December 24 and Luke 24, you are celebrating not only our Savior's birth but the greatest gift of all—His death and resurrection.

—Carole Leathem, speaker and author of *Finding Joy in My Messy Life*

Looking for a convenient Bible study to inspire your faith during Advent? Christine Trimpe's warm, friendly voice will guide you through quick and easy lessons, perfect for the busy Christmas season. You'll be filled with greater joy as you go through the chapters with a warm cup of cocoa and your Bible.

—Sarah Geringer, Christian speaker, podcaster, artist, creative coach, and author of several books, including *Christmas Peace for Busy Moms*

In Christine Trimpe's *Seeking Joy through the Gospel of Luke*, you will find solace, comfort, and, yes, *joy* through the comparison she makes between God's amazing Word via the letter of Luke and our own struggles through life's most challenging circumstances. She will lead you down a path day by day through the Gospel of Luke, which will culminate in a wondrous gift—a season of great joy! Christine has been inspired by the Holy Spirit to share her journey of joy, and you won't want to miss this one-of-a-kind devotional written by someone who has been there and struggled through some of life's toughest storms herself.

—J. C. Lafler, speaker and author of *Finding Joy*

Jingle all the way to Christmas day! In *Seeking Joy through the Gospel of Luke*, Christine Trimpe takes us on a true joy-seeking adventure even in the most difficult of chapters. She recognizes this season can be hard for so many and gives us such a gift to purposefully find joy. This journey with Jesus is the reminder we all need of the ultimate joy and reason for this season.

—Samantha J. Morgan, founder of Rush to Hope Ministries and author of *Miraculously My Own: One Woman's Incredible Journey of Infertility, Faith, and Adoption*

In a time when the world is weary and worn out from so much sad, depressing news, this devotional is the medicine that will soothe the soul. Christine not only shows her own vulnerability but explains how Luke and others felt during their walk with Jesus. With her beautiful way of telling the story, excellent questions, and guided prayers, you will be waking each morning with joy to share another day with prayer first. I can't think of a better way to spend the Christmas season than by reading this encouraging devotional. Christine makes you feel as if you are sharing a warm cup of coffee and having girlfriend Bible study. You will enjoy learning about the story of Luke and going deeper in your faith. I will look forward to keeping this book on my coffee table this winter.

—Phylis Mantelli, speaker, coach, and author of *Unmothered: Life with a Mom Who Couldn't Love Me* and co-host of the Podcast *24 Carat Conversations*

Are you ready to rediscover the joy of the Lord amid wearying circumstances? My friend Christine Trimpe ignites unspeakable joy as she invites you into the biblical account of Jesus's birth and sacrificial death through the Gospel of Luke. Christine's love for God's Word and her joy in Christ shine through in this insightful Advent devotional!

—Cheryl Lutz is an inspirational speaker, Bible teacher, lay counselor, and the founder of Securely Held Ministries

Seeking
JOY
through the Gospel of Luke

Merry Christmas dear Jessica! 2021

Seeking
JOY
through the Gospel of Luke

A CHRISTMAS TO CALVARY
ADVENT COUNTDOWN

Thank you for sharing the Good News of great joy with me!
With Joy!
Christine Trimpe
Luke 2:19 ♡

Christine Trimpe

REDEMPTION PRESS

Published by Redemption Press, PO Box 427, Enumclaw, WA 98022
Toll-Free (844) 2REDEEM (273-3336)

Redemption Press is honored to present this title in partnership with the author. The views expressed or implied in this work are those of the author. Redemption Press provides our imprint seal representing design excellence, creative content, and high-quality production.

Cover and Author Photos by Sarah Wyatt-Stahl, You and Eye Photography, Berkley, Michigan. All images used with permission.

Quotes from Patricia Durgin, Adam Groh, and Lori Boruff are used with permission.

ISBN 13: 978-1-64645-433-4 (Paperback)
978-1-64645-434-1 (ePub)
978-1-64645-432-7 (Mobi)

Library of Congress Catalog Card Number: 2021920886

DEDICATION

To my family: Rob, Kyle, Kaitlin, and Mike. You were there before I found my passion and the true meaning of joy. I'm not quite sure how you put up with me all those years. Your encouragement and prodding to share this joy-fueled journey with the world inspired these words to pour out from my heart. I can't thank you or love you enough.

CONTENTS

FOREWORD

Every year there is the "it" gift. The latest gaming system, electronic, air fryer, or toy. People scatter to stores far and wide and search every website to find one in stock. If you're lucky or want to pay $1,200 for a PS5 (or does anyone remember the Cabbage Patch craze in the 1980s?), you find your golden goose, wrap it real nice, and put it under the tree.

Here is the problem with "it" gifts—nearly all of them end up in the trash or giveaway pile within a few years. Your "it" will end up in a garbage pit.

Yet the process repeats over and over every year.

Reality is there is only one "it" gift that never fades, breaks, doesn't fit properly, or goes out of fashion—the Word of God! It is in the Word that you will discover the Gift who brings life, hope, and *joy*. That gift is Jesus.

Christine has "it" because she has Him. Her love for the Word of God is infectious and inspiring.

> Blessed is the one who does not walk in step with the wicked or stand in the way that sinners take or sit in the company of mockers, but whose *delight is in the law of the Lord*, and who meditates on his law day and night. That person is like a tree planted by streams of water, which yields its fruit in season and whose leaf does not wither—whatever they do prospers. (Psalm 1:1–3, emphasis mine)

When your delight is in the life-giving law of the Lord, you *find joy*—exceedingly great joy. You are like a tree planted near streams of water. Your roots grow deep, your leaves shine, and your branches bear fruit. Or in other words, as you linger in the Word and let the Spirit root your faith, your tangible relationship with the Lord shines and you bear fruit of love, joy, peace, forbearance, kindness, goodness, faithfulness, gentleness, and self-control.

So many settle for knockoff gifts. These are gifts that promise big and deliver little. The Word promises hope and delivers joy. *Seeking Joy through the Gospel of Luke* will help you sift through the knockoffs and find the real joy-giving Jesus.

As a ministry couple, we are amazed at what God has done through Christine's speaking and writing. She is an inspiration because she loves God's inspired Word with a passion.

We whole-heartedly encourage you to create some space and spend time reading Luke and reflecting with Christine this Christmas season.

After the seasons we have been through these last few years, we all need joy. The Word has made it so clear how we find this joy. Jesus says in John 15 to abide in Him so that your *joy* may be full. This is what Jesus wants for you.

Do not settle for another "it" gift. Delight in the Word and find joy that lasts!

Pastor Adam and Jennifer Groh
Berkley Community Church
Berkley, Michigan

Acknowledgments

I'm blessed to have a deeper understanding of gratefulness in recent years as I walked through my joy-filled transformation story with Jesus. For many years, I never knew I was seeking joy and took the blessings in my life for granted. Recently, I've learned gratefulness goes way beyond the politeness and good manners my parents taught me.

Now as I consider who to thank as I prepare to launch my first published book, the depth of my gratitude leaves me speechless. But I'm a writer now (as I've been told by all my writing pals), so I'll proceed and pray I don't leave anyone out.

First and most importantly, I give all the praise, honor, and glory to Jesus—He is restoring, renewing, and constantly redeeming my walk with Him which fills me with unspeakable joy every day. I'm honored to take this unspeakable feeling in the depths of my soul and spread the good news of His great joy everywhere I go. Sharing this message at Christmastime is a special blessing indeed. I've always loved Christmas, even all those years I neglected and glossed over the miracle of the season.

My husband, Robert Trimpe, has been my biggest cheerleader and rock all these crazy good and sometimes hard years. I don't think I've ever loved him so much as on the day when he finally agreed that it was time for me to quit my corporate career to pursue this unexpected calling of writing, speaking, and coaching. Again, words are inadequate to express my heart—let's just say, Rob, I love you, and you will always have my whole heart.

To my wonderful children, Kyle and Kaitlin, plus my awesome son-in-law, Mike Bratby. I'm sorry for those years I was crabby and exhausted. I hope I've made up for those years in showing you the meaning of abundant joy when you walk with Jesus. Thank you for not giving up on me. I love you all.

To my parents, Ken and Georgia Halloran. They instilled in me a love for Christmas. It was festive, it created memories, and it contributed to a solid foundation of faith. Thanks Mom and Dad for raising me in a loving Christian home so that after my years of wandering, I could return to the faith of my family.

Just the other day, I sat with my lifelong friends with tears in my eyes and tried to explain (like I said, unspeakable joy) exactly how much their support means to me. These girls have been by my side for decades. They've seen me at my worst, and they're celebrating with me the best years in this exciting writing journey. Everyone should be blessed with lifelong friends from childhood. Thank you Cyndi, Dee-Dee, Dianne, Heidi, Jill, and Theresa.

God has truly blessed me with many friends in this season of life. Friends who pray, friends who cheer, friends who cry with me, friends who teach me new things, friends who want me to teach them new things (hah!), friends who encourage, friends who randomly send cards in the mail, and friends who bring me bacon. Many of these dear friends were found in my local church, my favorite place to connect. Too many to name, but thank you to those special friends at Berkley Community Church.

A very special thanks to my incredible pastor and his lovely wife, Pastor Adam and Jennifer Groh. You have blessed me immensely by contributing to this book by writing the Foreword. As Jennifer likes to say, "Love you much!" Back at you both.

Special shout out to Sarah Wyatt-Stahl of *You and Eye Photography* for the cover photo and headshots for this project. Your enthusiasm in freezing cold weather to get the perfect shot before the snow landed in my face will always be remembered with laughter and sincere admiration. Your photography skills amaze me.

In this writing journey, I have been blessed to connect with amazing women like my marketing coach Patricia Durgin. She gets ministry life and teaches me new things from her years of experience. A very special thank-you to her for helping me brainstrom the title of this book. Picture the two of us doing a happy dance on the day the Lord revealed the gift of joy in the happy and the hard from Christmas through Calvary!

To my Coffee Crew and event planners, Shannon and Jenn, who share my passion for morning coffee. Thank you for helping me plan the best Christmas events and for your constant prayers and guidance when I start getting way ahead of myself and the Lord.

To the most supportive community of writers and speakers—I appreciate you all. In particular sisters in SIS (Sisters in Seasons), AWSA (Advanced Writers and Speakers Association), CCC (Christian Communicators Conference), and the SWFH (She Writes for Him) Tribe. Special thanks to author and speaker, Page Geske, for being my "last supper" friend at She Speaks Studio 2018 and pushing me along this writing path since the day we met. I treasure all your friendships.

Eternal gratitude to Olivia Dixon. With her godly wisdom, she helped me address the overwhelming stress in my life. She reminded me boundaries are healthy when I started to spiral in my type-A bent to do *all the things* and keep everyone happy at the expense of my health. Olivia gave me the push I needed to fully trust in God and leave behind excessive stress in my life to pursue my passion and care for my family first. Everyone needs an Olivia in their corner.

My website visitors are the best. It's delightful to hear from you and know you support this ministry to spread the good news of God's healing touch in every aspect of our being—body, mind, and spirit. Thank you for joining me in this joy-fueled journey. And thank you for knocking my socks off last Christmas with all your interest in the *Christmas Countdown Through the Book of Luke.* You are the reason this book is in print. A million thanks.

Kudos and high fives to the team at Redemption Press who worked on this project not just with me but for me and the message God has for readers in this Christmas season. Athena, Dori, Cynthia, Jennifer, and Stephanie––many thanks for your patience and teaching me how this little thing called "publishing a book" gets done. I'm so glad you said, "Yes!" to this manuscript. Oh, and to Carole! We just met and instantly bonded over joy. I'm excited to walk this joy journey with you.

A heartfelt thanks to those of you who supported the funding of this book. It's because of you that this story of the *good news of great joy* will reach hungry souls for many Christmas seasons to come. God bless the following supporters, advocates, and promoters: Stephanie Hull, Aunt Betty Halloran, Carole Leathem, Denise Jewell, Teresa Moyer, Shelly Brown, Patricia Maslowsky, Heidi Moyer, Aunt Ellen Anderson, Amy L. Harden, Dianne Larson, Connie Lee Barron, Teresa Smith, Debbie Alsdorf, and Annette Cotterell. And thank you for those of you who continued to financially support this project after these pages went to print.

One final but extra special mention to my dear friends, the Keefe family. My lifelong friends, Dee-Dee and Bill, along with their kids Cara, Erin, and Lily, made an extra-special effort as a family to partner with me in spreading the gospel message for many years to come. I am overwhelmed by your very generous contribution and love you and your giving hearts. You know I'm a sap, so pass me a tissue.

Love to each of you from the bottom of my joy-filled heart.
Christine Trimpe

INTRODUCTION

Why Seek Joy and How to Use This Advent Countdown Devotional

If you had told me five short years ago that I'd be writing to you about joy, I would have laughed in your face. Despite my happy façade, I would be the last person to speak about unspeakable joy. Although I was raised in the church, I would best define my former relationship with Jesus as casual and my understanding of joy as confused.

But God. He has a way of lifting the fog of confusion for His chosen daughters. That's you and me. He recently brought me through a healing journey, which is almost unbelievable—kind of like a Christmas miracle, and daily He is restoring my body, renewing my mind, and redeeming my walk with Him.

The result? Joy. Remarkable and unspeakable joy. I get it now. It was there all along, I just didn't know where or how to find it until the day God picked me up from the pit and I picked up His Word. At first, digging into my Bible probably looked like a discipline, but quickly reading God's Word first thing every morning turned into my daily delight. It is truly the one thing in my daily routine that satisfies my soul.

And so the process of burying the joy, which I had lacked for decades, deep into every fiber of my being began and continues daily. It's a good thing He gifted me this joy because the storms of life were about to hit hard—He knew I would need it. This devotional was written as therapy for my battered soul as I battled against the stress of three difficult trials. I call this season of my life the "trifecta of the perfect storm."

Initially I wrote for myself, but God clearly inspired me through promptings of the Holy Spirit to share this message of joy because the world is hurting. It's so easy to see the pain and struggles we experience during the Christmas season. We want to feel "good tidings of great joy," but what do we do with our pain? Can Jesus relate to this pain? And even if we've had a particularly joy-filled year, how can we be sensitive to others' pain during this season? What does God have to teach us about joy to share with others during this advent time?

God captured my attention with a repetitive phrase we all know from the Christmas hymn "O Holy Night." This song happens to be my favorite song to hear and sing during the season. But it started running through my mind in early November (way before we even made it through Thanksgiving).

The *weary* world rejoices; the weary world *rejoices*. That phrase kept repeating over and over, and the only thing I could really say was, "Oh yes, Lord. We *are* weary. We crave joy and peace at Christmastime. What am I supposed to do with this?"

It didn't take long before it dawned on me, "Hey, I know something about joy and rejoicing. In fact, I blog about it every December as I countdown to Christmas through the Gospel of Luke." That's when the Lord prompted me to write even more . . . to go on a joy-seeking adventure to find where joy is woven throughout every story of this gospel. His plan for my lengthy blog posts was to point everyone to Jesus, who is the reason for the season, and I just followed His lead by diving into Scripture while seeking the places where joy cropped up. It's remarkable what He revealed to me in even the toughest passages.

God's plan for salvation is revealed through the fulfillment of Old Testament prophecies throughout the entire Gospel of Luke. Starting in chapter one, Luke mentions his purpose for writing this gospel:

Many have undertaken to draw up an account of the things that have been fulfilled among us, just as they were handed down to us by those who from the first were eyewitnesses and servants of the word. With this in mind, since I myself

have carefully investigated everything from the beginning,
I too decided to write an orderly account for you, most
excellent Theophilus, so that you may know the certainty
of the things you have been taught. (Luke 1:1–4)

It is amazing how Luke wrote this letter all those many years ago so that a Roman believer named Theophilus would be certain of the things Luke had been taught about Jesus, and little did Luke know it would be for us, too, thousands of years later. Through the pages of Luke, we will seek and find joy in chapter 1 starting on December 1. And we will read about joy in chapter 24 on December 24 and in every chapter in between. Even in the painful parts on Calvary, there is joy to be found as Luke wraps his entire gospel message in a big bow with the promise of joy. We will find over and over again a great truth: the Christmas season is a season of *great joy*. I can't think of a better Christmas gift!

A long time ago, there was an American evangelist named Billy Sunday, known for being a preacher you didn't need a dictionary to understand, and here's what he had to say about joy: "If you have no joy in your religion, there's a leak in your Christianity somewhere."[1]

Friend, during this Christmas season, let's not overlook this gift of joy. Instead of leaking out from our lack of delighting in our Christian walk, let's start seeking joy so we can confidently share the *good news of great joy* to all mankind. Now more than ever, the world needs this joy, and Christmas offers a wonderful opportunity when those in need are most receptive.

To get started, let me give you some simple instructions. Beginning on December 1, we have twenty-four days to journey together through this devotional. Each day, I suggest you read the corresponding chapter in Luke first and *then* read the devotional. Each chapter ends with some questions to ponder and respond to and wraps up with a short, guided prayer. I've also prepared a printable advent calendar for you with highlights from each chapter to display during the countdown. (See the link to download in the *Seeking Joy Resources* in the back of the book.)

Follow this process each day. As we move along seeking joy in the Christmas to Calvary story in Luke, I think you will find that joy will overflow in abundance from your heart like it does mine. Let's get going.

Be joy-fueled,

Christine Trimpe

When Elizabeth heard Mary's greeting, the baby leaped in her womb, and Elizabeth was filled with the Holy Spirit. In a loud voice she exclaimed: "Blessed are you among women, and blessed is the child you will bear! But why am I so favored, that the mother of my Lord should come to me?" As soon as the sound of your greeting reached my ears, the baby in my womb leaped for joy.

Luke 1:41–44

JOY BREAKS THE SILENCE

Breathless anticipation fills my heart and soul during advent every year. Can you feel it too? The excitement building over another season of *great joy*. Sure, as a child it was all about the presents. And now, of course, it's all about *His presence*. It's like hearing an old story told over and over again, and it just keeps getting better.

What's in store for us in Luke's gospel story this advent season, God?

From staring at the pile of gifts under the sparkle of my childhood Christmas trees to seeing the wonder and awe in my own children's eyes, I'm now in this season of grown children and the quiet stillness of a nearly empty house. I'm sipping coffee and settling into another good story in His Word, always asking, "What's in store, Lord?" I will never tire of this.

But I am tired. Tired of this year. Tired of watching my friends and family struggling to make sense of the chaos in our culture. Tired of the struggles in my own home. Another Christmas season arrives, and I'm asking the Lord, "God, what's in store?"

I've been thinking a lot about the four hundred years of silence between the Old and New Testament stories of the Bible. Wow, there were so many faithful servants of God, generations of them, wondering the whereabouts of God. Comparing this to our present-day sufferings, let's pause and imagine a silence from God lasting four hundred years? A deafening silence offers us great perspective.

So, I eagerly anticipate this journey through the Gospel of Luke each year. Luke picks up after those years of silence with some themes we desperately need in this season, especially the highlight of this devotional's mission: joy. I don't know about you, but I need to constantly seek joy so I'm not sinking in the events happening around the world and in my own circle.

A little secret about me . . . I'm a checklist checkity-checker, type A, calendar-loving gal who loves a plan, and I don't generally pencil in confusing world events and family hardships in my annual to-do list. So when I'm overwhelmed, I ask again, "Lord, what's in store?"

What a relief to find His plan in Luke 1 where we start today. There are so many lessons packed in this long chapter, but right from the beginning, we see that Luke wrote this Gospel to strengthen the faith of all believers (vv. 1–4). I don't know about you, but I sense that we all need an extra dose of strength today with a whole lot of joy to carry us through.

In verses 5 through 28, we find joy in the conception of John the Baptist to an elderly Zechariah and Elizabeth. Imagine this barren and faithful couple's overwhelming joy in hearing this news. The angel Gabriel announced that John's birth would bring great joy to his parents and that many people would rejoice over his birth.

But do not miss what happened to Zechariah when he doubted this joyous news from Gabriel by asking, "How can I be sure of this?" (v. 18).

Gabriel responded: "And now you will be silent and not able to speak until the day this happens, *because you did not believe my words,* which will come true at their appointed time" (v. 20, emphasis mine).

Because of his unbelief, Gabriel muted Zechariah. The proper time was fulfilled further along in the chapter (vv. 57–66). Zechariah was able to speak again, and his first response was praise to God (v. 64). Their community even rejoiced with them over the birth of John. I love that their neighbors and relatives shared in their joy. There is no room for gossip and jealousy when God is working His plan. What a joy-filled and joy-fulfilled scene that left this community in awe!

In the miraculous account of Mary's story, we witness her encounter with the angel Gabriel in verses 26 through 38 with a joyful willing heart. Mary was chosen to be the mother of the Son of God. Can you imagine? As Gabriel greeted her with the puzzling news, her response inquired of him to provide a deeper understanding of God's plan for her life, not of doubt, just wonder.

"How will this be," Mary asked the angel, "since I am a virgin?" (v. 34). Fair question, don't you think?

Mary embraced this news with the heart of the Lord's servant (v. 38) and hurried off to share her good news with Elizabeth. How special this reunion must have been with both women overflowing with joy from the Lord. Even the unborn John leaped for joy in the womb when he was in the presence of the unborn Jesus (v. 41). Picture this meeting of Elizabeth and Mary. I notice a joyful and heartfelt time of sisterhood—so much joy resulting in so much praise and worship of the God who was revealing His plan of good news.

This seems like a great time to rejoice in a song of praise (vv. 46–55). As we anticipate the birth of Christ and hunger for peace and joy, we can appreciate the heart of Mary in her song: "He has filled the hungry with good things" (v. 53).

After all those years of silence, these faithful and obedient servants of God were no doubt hungry for some good news.

Through my journey of physical, emotional, and spiritual healing, I recognized the depths and depravity of my hunger. I realize that I craved all the wrong things to satisfy my soul, which can leave a gal bone weary and in desperate need of some good news.

Today I testify to all the good things He fills me with, and it's not food. I'm grateful for the blessing of His joy and the ability to choose joy every day in all circumstances. That's the satiating goodness I choose. Even in my weariness, I celebrate these lyrics down in my soul: "The weary world rejoices."

What a great start in our joy-seeking journey. Right from the beginning, we glean that the Gospel of Luke is a wonderful reminder of the promises of God's plan to bring joy to the world. You may be weary and worn out, but as you spend time seeking joy in His Word every day this Christmas season, you will soon rejoice. And I just bet it will change your perspective a wee bit and leave you with breathless anticipation!

Ponderings

As you sit in the silence with God, identify some struggles or hardships you face today. Recall while reading in Luke 1 that Zechariah asked doubtful questions and ended up mute, while Mary asked insightful questions to gain a deeper understanding. What kind of questions are you asking God? Are they the right questions?

Finding Joy

After centuries of silence, we find faithful servants of Christ ready and willing to participate in the greatest story ever told, which was unfolding before their eyes. Joy, wonder, and celebration are in the opening words of the Christmas story.

Prayer

Heavenly Father, thank You for Your Word and Your promises fulfilled through Scripture and the Gospel of Luke today. Thank You for the gift of joy and for setting the story in Luke with this miraculous gift. Help me to receive this gift with a willing servant's heart. Give me wisdom to ask the right questions today. I rejoice in this story of *good news of great joy* and will celebrate in this joyous Christmas season with everyone I interact with today. Amen.

An angel of the Lord appeared to them, and the glory of the Lord shone around them, and they were terrified. But the angel said to them, "Do not be afraid. I bring you good news that will cause *great joy* for all the people."

Luke 2:9–10 (emphasis mine)

HAVE NO FEAR— JOY IS HERE!

Be truthful. Would you be able to identify three things today causing you anxiety or keeping you awake for hours during the night counting sheep? I sure can.

Set that aside for a moment. Can you recall a startling moment? Something so unexpected you jump out of your seat with your heart pounding? Yeah, we've all had those moments, too.

Today, let's put ourselves in the company of the shepherds we find nearby in the fields.

"An angel of the Lord appeared to them, and the glory of the Lord shone around them, and *they were terrified*" (v. 9, emphasis mine).

Wow, imagine—those poor shepherds were minding their own business, tending to their flocks, and *Wham!* Angels everywhere! Scripture says they were terrified. Just going about their business, these shepherds find themselves major players in the greatest story ever told. They certainly could use some comfort from this angel.

"But the angel said to them, 'Do not be afraid. I bring you *good news of great joy* that will be for all the people. Today in the town of David a Savior has been born to you; He is Christ the Lord'" (vv. 10–11, emphasis mine).

Considering these terrified shepherds, sometimes I wonder what would have happened if they had chosen to run for the hills. I mean, come on, admit it, if this happened to you today, what might be your first instinct? I'll tell you my truth! In my past, I most definitely would have run to hide. I did it for decades.

I have some terrifying truths in my past—fear of rejection, isolation, humiliation, judgment, comparison, and being the topic of gossip. I was never in a hurry to put myself in the middle of fear. Instead, I remained paralyzed and ineffective in sharing the *good news.*

I picture those fears I mentioned as a huge brick wall that kept me on the other side of finding joy in my life.

Sure, I believed, but I was never obedient, nor did I have a willing heart to respond like the shepherds.

"So they hurried off and found Mary and Joseph, and the baby, who was lying in the manger" (v. 16, emphasis mine).

They hurried off. They were excited. And they responded in obedience to their role in the story. The result? They returned to their calling while glorifying and praising the Lord (v. 20). Look at the amazing testimony they left behind. I can imagine the stories they told to their friends and family—and, most likely, even complete strangers.

These lowly shepherds were the first to share this *good news of great joy* to the amazement of all who would listen. And what was Mary feeling as she witnessed these events? Let's look into the heart of this momma.

"But Mary *treasured up* all these things and *pondered* them in her heart" (v. 19, emphasis mine).

Oh, this verse fills my own heart with awe and wonder. Indeed, the questions at the end of each chapter in this book require you to spend time pondering and treasuring the gifts of joy you find in this journey. I can't wrap my brain around the magnitude of being the mother of the Messiah. How about you? I wonder—was Mary frightened? Overwhelmed? Full of anxiety? Or was she full of peace and joy in her quiet reflection? Let's dive a little deeper in the verse.

From *Strong's Greek Concordance,* we learn that *treasured up* from the Greek word *suntéreó* means to keep close, to preserve. And one definition of *pondered* from the Greek word *symballousa* translates as "to consider."[2]

I envision Mary being contemplative and careful in her response to this miracle occurring in her life. I imagine her intently storing the details of this event to remember and reflect in the future on this moment of her child's life. She didn't have the benefit of scrapbooks and cell phone cameras, but I believe she was blessed with these images to last a lifetime.

Unlike me, Mary's heart wasn't positioned to run and hide from the things that kept me in the dark for years: rejection, isolation, humiliation, judgment, comparison, and being the topic of gossip.

Verse 19 speaks volumes of peace in the simple and beautiful description by Luke. Mary keeps all this close in her heart, and that's what we can emulate. Peace and joy. Calm from the chaos. Reflecting and pondering. Put yourself in that moment, sister. Just breathe and trust; there is no room at the inn for fear.

Be encouraged through the joy we find today in God's Word. He sent an angel to tell these shepherds, "Have no fear; joy is here." Surely, He is fulfilling this promise to you today.

In times of uncertainty, remember that God is nearby. And He delivers through a great company of heavenly host proclaiming:

"Glory to God in the highest heaven, and on earth peace to those on whom his favor rests" (v. 14).

May you find true peace and joy as you live, like the shepherds, nearby His Word every day.

Ponderings

Is there anything in your life causing you panic, anxiety, and fear? Identify the source(s) and write a promise of peace and joy over each circumstance.

When the shepherds returned to their community, they were filled with the great joy the angels told them about. In response, they shared the good news with everyone. What does great joy look like to you? When is the last time you shared the *good news of great joy* with someone? How can you do this today?

Finding Joy

The shepherds fear turned to joy. Their joy emboldened them to spread the word about Jesus. Mary held this miraculous story close to her mother's heart with great joy.

Prayer

Heavenly Father, thank You for Your bold announcement through a company of angels to the shepherds in the field nearby my newborn Savior. Thank You for their bold witness and their worship. I pray for this level of courage to share today Your *good news of great joy* to the lost and hurting. I pray for hearts and minds to be open and receptive during this Christmas season. And give me a joyful heart like Mary, to ponder and appreciate the beauty of this eternal Christmas gift. Amen.

And a voice from heaven said, "You are my dearly loved Son, and you bring me great joy."

Luke 3:22 NLT

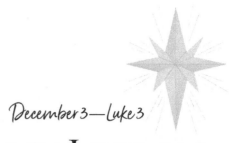

FINDING JOY IN THE GENEALOGY OF JESUS

My mom has been busy in recent years documenting our family ancestry all the way back to the passengers on the Mayflower ship that landed at Plymouth Rock in 1620. It's taken many hours of hard work to prove this genealogy.

Her diligence has paid off though! On the day before Thanksgiving, much to her joy and delight, she received a confirmation from the Mayflower Society that her documentation had enough sources and would be processed. Our entire extended family rejoiced in this special and timely holiday news.

Such a discovery fills me with awe and so many questions. How cool would it be to sit with my Mayflower Fuller family and hear their stories? I cannot comprehend their trials and tribulations as they crossed the Atlantic Ocean in a crude sailing vessel to finally reach their new home after roughly two miserable months. Would we be able to muster this courage? I don't know.

I wonder, did the faith which prompted them to seek freedom from religious oppression truly stick through so many generations to trickle down to me? I like to think that my great (times fourteen) grandparents would find joy in their legacy of faith.

Imagine the ancient Israelites wandering through all those generations with no word from God. As John the Baptist was preparing the way for the maturity of Jesus's ministry on earth, the people he influenced and baptized began to ask John, "What should we do?" (vv. 10, 12, and 14). They wanted to be ready and, in fact, were expectantly waiting on the Christ (v. 15). Could it be? The long-awaited Messiah? Joy to the world!

After so many years of silence, those people were becoming impatient or perhaps they were bouncing off the walls in excitement. Scripture tells us they were so anxious that they began assuming that perhaps John the Baptist might be the Messiah (v. 15). They missed a few details from their Scripture lessons pointing them where to look for the true Messiah. I bet they nodded off during the oral readings in the genealogy lessons. Let's dig in and discover what they overlooked.

In verses 23 through 38, I counted the generations myself but wanted to be accurate. The full genealogy from Adam to Jesus was seventy-six clearly listed generations, and from Noah to Jesus, sixty-six generations.[3]

Do you gloss over the genealogies in Scripture? I confess that I used to skim through the so and so beget so and so. But as I enjoy my family lineage (thanks to my mom's dedication to her hobby), I now seek joy in the lineage of Jesus because it is absolutely amazing, right?

I really took note of this genealogy in Luke chapter 3 today. No longer will I skip over these passages. A voice from heaven announced the importance of this little detail and we should pay attention.

> One day when the crowds were being baptized, Jesus Himself was baptized. As he was praying, the heavens opened, and the Holy Spirit, in bodily form, descended on him like a dove. And a voice from heaven said, "You are my dearly loved Son, and you bring me *great joy*." (vv. 21–22 NLT, emphasis mine)

That's the voice of one proud Father.

This is where I find the joy in today's chapter. God planned this moment from the beginning of time. Do you think His joy was over-flowing as His plan came to fruition? I sure do.

If you are seeking more information on the story of Jesus, I invite you to accept this truth from a most important verse written by John: "For God so loved the world that he gave his one and only Son, that whoever believes in him shall not perish but have eternal life" (John 3:16).

There's your invitation to the family party. "Whoever"—that means you. When you accept this truth, you become part of God's family as His adopted child—part of Jesus's spiritual lineage forever. That's something to really rejoice about.

And from those of us already adopted into the family of God, we are waiting for you to join us! Imagine the family reunion that will take place in heaven. I expect it will feel like a festive Christmas every day. Now that's a sure celebration of great joy.

Ponderings

Reflect on your own family heritage. Whether your lineage is Christian or not, write a short memory of an event that brings you joyful memories.

In verse 18, John exhorts the people and preaches the good news to them. As you engage your friends and family this Christmas season, how might you use a story to lovingly exhort others to find the joy in this Christmas season? Pay attention to the doors God may be opening for you to share. Who is He putting on your mind?

Finding Joy

Despite our earthly family situation, we can rest assured in the joy of being an adopted child in the eternal family of God. And God, our Father in heaven, wants us to know that we are His dearly loved children and that we bring Him great joy.

Prayer

Heavenly Father, on the days we have a sense of not belonging anywhere or to any particular family, meet us and remind us of our inheritance in Your family. Be near and guide us as we walk this journey on earth while we patiently wait for our heavenly family reunion. Thank you for this invitation to be with You for eternity. Amen.

"The Spirit of the Lord is on me, because he has anointed me to proclaim good news to the poor. He has sent me to proclaim freedom for the prisoners and recovery of sight for the blind, to set the oppressed free, to proclaim the year of the Lord's favor."

Luke 4:18–19

The Joy of the Lord's Favor

We live in a time when we can't always count on the information we receive. Headlines that sell are often outrageous, overly exaggerated, and potentially full of fake news. If we're not careful, what the media giants are selling us can rob us of our joy and lead us down a miserable path of despair.

Today in Luke 4, we witness Jesus making waves and making news. Now this is news we can use. Yesterday we witnessed the people buzzing around with the idea that they may be living in the history of the long-awaited Messiah. Picture them sharing the word on the street. How exciting!

Now we learn how Jesus finally begins His earthly ministry in a public way. He's walking out the journey His Father set out before Him. In just this one chapter the narrative bounces back and forth from amazement to fury and back to amazement.

My favorite part of this chapter is the scene in verses 16 through 30. The setting is in the synagogue in Nazareth, where Jesus had been brought up. This is His hometown, the place of His childhood friends and family—all who had watched Him grow up. If you've ever lived in a small town, like me, you know everyone knows your name (and your business).

Jesus was handed a scroll and read the following, which originated in Isaiah 61:

"The Spirit of the Lord is on me, because he has anointed me to preach *good news* to the poor. He has sent me to proclaim freedom for the prisoners and recovery of sight for the blind, to set the oppressed free, to proclaim the year of the Lord's favor." (vv. 18–19, emphasis mine)

Joy to the world! Let's go further into the scene: "Then he rolled up the scroll, gave it back to the attendant and sat down. *The eyes of everyone in the synagogue were fastened on him*" (v. 20, emphasis mine).

Mesmerizing.

And then He continued, "Today this scripture is fulfilled in your hearing" (v. 21).

Mic drop.

Imagine the buzz this created in the crowd:

"Uh, what did He just say?"

"Is this Joseph's son? Joseph of Nazareth?" they wondered in disbelief.

Luke records that His fellow citizens of Nazareth were amazed by the gracious words flowing from Jesus's mouth. But surely their minds were confounded by the passage from the prophet Isaiah that He just read to them. Was this hometown boy anointed by the Spirit of the Lord? Was Jesus saying He was the one meant to set prisoners free and restore sight to the blind? Release the oppressed? And what in the world does "proclaim the year of the Lord's favor" even mean?

Jesus knew what they were thinking and responded to their unspoken questions by saying, "Surely you will quote this proverb to me: 'Physician, heal yourself!' And you will tell me, 'Do here in your hometown what we have heard that you did in Capernaum.' Truly I tell you," he continued, "no prophet is accepted in his hometown" (vv. 23–24).

Wow, my heart breaks for Jesus. What joy robbers. They had the long-awaited Messiah in their midst, but they weren't willing to believe the prophesy in Isaiah could be fulfilled in this hometown boy unless He performed signs and miracles for them like He'd done in

Capernaum. Because of their unbelief, Jesus condemned them. Their furious response to his condemnation drove Jesus out of town with the intent to kill Him. How shocking!

Perhaps a sensational news headline read: "Strange vagabond returns to Nazareth, challenges learned scholars—narrowly escapes death."

Amazement. Fury. Then what?

Jesus went back to Capernaum, specifically to Galilee. There He was received and welcomed by the townspeople because His message carried authority (vv. 31–32). Here He fulfilled His calling of proclaiming good news to reach the poor, the hungry, the sick, the lowest of the low. And those who welcomed His power and authority began to spread the news about Him far and wide (vv. 36–37).

An alternative news headline might read: "Son of God heals the sick, shares good news with forgotten people—streets are filled with jubilation."

And we are back to amazement. Herein we discover the joy.

There are days when I can't avoid the news and a pit of despair rises in my gut. But through my own joyful journey of healing my body, mind, and spirit, I've learned to cling to joy. As I continue on this path of transformation and sanctification, I want to tell you the number one source of my hope and joy is straight from the Word of God.

If I had not finally found the daily delight of digging into God's Word first thing every day . . . well, honestly, I believe the scope of my trials and weariness, plus the chaotic news and world events would have knocked me off my feet and wrecked me emotionally and physically. So, I praise Jesus with all that I am for my timely healing.

I'm overjoyed that you are here reading God's Word every day. When the world around you feels furious, let's remember to always choose joy and choose to live in the promises of the Lord's favor.

Ponderings

Just like Jesus, sometimes you know deep down that you are not welcome in your own hometown. A modern-day example could be finding yourself in the midst of people who don't think or believe the same way you do. How would that make you feel (e.g., lonely, isolated, and afraid)?

When confronting such a scenario, how might you walk through the unfriendly crowd like Jesus did while leaving evidence of the joy He wants you to share?

Finding Joy

We can rejoice in the fact that the anointed Son of God, Jesus, came to this earth to preach the good news. From this *good news of great joy,* we find favor in the Lord and celebrate this Christmas season the true news of our freedom in Him.

Prayer

Heavenly Father, when devasting and confusing news surrounds us every day in this world, remind us of the *good news of great joy* in the birth of Your Son. Thank You for this miraculous and beautiful gift of His virgin birth and ministry on earth to set me, a captive, free. Amen.

Everyone was amazed and gave praise to God. They were *filled with awe* and said, "We have seen *remarkable things* today."

Luke 5:26 (emphasis mine)

JOYFUL HEALING

I have a remarkable story to share with you today. The story where Jesus heals the paralytic in Luke 5:17–26.

In today's chapter, we find Jesus in a home teaching a crowd. And we find a group of good friends desperately trying to get their paralytic friend in front of the feet of Jesus, knowing that He would heal him. It took some ingenuity, but they succeeded. Their faith on display touched Jesus, and he declared, "Friend, your sins are forgiven" (v. 20).

Part of my story is so relatable to these verses, as I, too, was paralyzed by fear and my poor health. Living for decades as morbidly obese weighed heavily on me, not only physically but emotionally and spiritually too. My lifestyle stole my joy. My witness for Jesus was nonexistent.

My closest friends are wonderful, and I love them dearly, but these friends of mine couldn't lift the weight of my mat. Yes, they are encouraging and kind, but I never shared with them the depths of my pain and sorrow over my situation. Perhaps a little vulnerability would have sparked my journey a little sooner. Who knows? Truthfully, I never wanted to confront or talk about food addiction nor how I found comfort in hiding out and stuffing my feelings with addictive high carb foods. No one wants to talk about food addiction and the obvious set of circumstances I lived in.

For thirty years I traveled around a vicious cycle, trying to break free in my own power. I lived in chronic exhaustion, physically and mentally; I couldn't do the heavy lifting.

But you know who can? I know you've guessed Jesus. That's right.

Jesus did the heavy lifting. I often joke that it's a good thing He is strong, because He had to pick me up (and my one hundred excess pounds) from the lowest pit to set my feet on a firm rock.

The best part of my testimony? I had a deep longing in my heart to feel better. I had attempted weight loss over and over again for three decades in my own strength, and I failed over and over. I finally dropped all my struggles at His feet. I confessed my weaknesses, asked for healing, and also asked for an extra dose of His strength. In hindsight, I didn't realize all I was asking for. I just wanted to feel better, but He gifted me with so much more.

Coming back to Luke 5:21, the crowd of Pharisees immediately began to question the authority of Jesus and accused Him of blasphemy for claiming to be like God. Of course, because He was indeed God, Jesus had to explain to them that His acts of healing affirmed His power to forgive sins, too. That was another mic drop moment by Jesus.

Jesus then told the paralytic, "Get up, take your mat and go home" (v. 24). He stood up and went home praising God.

"Everyone was amazed and gave praise to God. They were *filled with awe* and said, 'We have seen *remarkable things* today'" (v. 26, emphasis mine).

I know a little bit about this *awe* and *remarkable things*. It's the source of my overflowing joy. It's no wonder after thirty years of trying and failing over and over again that I was worn out, weary, and hopeless to ever regain my health. It is remarkable He chose to heal me. I still pinch myself every day.

Truth be told, I still ask myself questions like, "Why me?" And I remind Jesus that I never deserved this gift of healing after living for so long ignoring a relationship with Him. This is grace.

For whatever reason, He took the tiny mustard seed of faith I had buried deep down in my soul and He nourished it. And it grew. And He started healing my body. He taught me that every single sacrifice was worth it. He taught me to trust. He taught me to armor up and battle against fear. He taught me that all these lessons served a purpose.

His purpose. And that's why I'm writing these words to share with you today.

And the sum of my daily abiding in Him through this journey? My heart overflows with abundant joy. This joyful journey of healing evolved into a ministry lifestyle that I refer to as *Joy-Fueled Living.* I say evolved because it sure takes a lot of work, and His work will never be done until He returns. But friend, the journey is so worth it, and the gift is unspeakable joy.

Your journey may be different. You may not struggle with obesity, but human nature lends to us stuffing ourselves with other worldly things, like shopping, gossiping, lying, and drinking, for example. Or how about just simply wasting time while not grounded in the Word daily? How will your joy grow and spread in serving Him and serving others until you pick up your mat and *walk*? It's Christmas . . . accept this gift of grace He offers so freely to you and rejoice.

Ponderings

Think about the actions of the friends and the paralytic. What's on your mat that you need to drop at the feet of Jesus?

Consider the response of Jesus to their faith—He healed and forgave their sins without hesitation. What does your expression of joy look like in the city streets? How could God use your story?

Finding Joy

Today we rejoice over the remarkable healing and forgiveness of sin that Jesus shares joyfully to those who seek Him in earnest faith.

Prayer

Heavenly Father, today I praise You for Your miracles. I'm grateful for the story of the healing of the paralytic and how it encourages me to pursue You at any cost. Today I examine the heaviness on my mat which weighs me down. I'm laying this burden at Your feet today and ask for Your forgiveness in carrying this load alone for too long. I rejoice in the freedom and will share Your joy today in this Christmas season of remarkable joy. Amen.

Today's Postscript:

I've maintained my weight loss for several years now, and recently I took a bold step to finally share about my struggles with food addiction. Friend, I know . . . no one wants to talk about this topic. Not even in the church. But I must share as an expression of the joy I've discovered in a healthy lifestyle He calls all of us to live. I'm honored to have a chapter in the compilation book from Redemption Press, *She Writes for Him: Stories of Living Hope.* My chapter *"Finding Freedom from Formidable Food"* is in the section on addiction. You can find more details and order a copy of this book on Amazon. Thanks for your support.

Rejoice in that day and leap for joy, because great is your reward in heaven.

Luke 6:23

December 6—Luke 6

JOY IN THE CHALLENGES

Pondering the Christmas season and story always builds a breathless anticipation in my spirit. As we move through the book of Luke, can you sense the wonder and awe of the people in that day as they witnessed firsthand all that was foretold and playing out before them?

Today Luke briefly introduces us, by name, to the twelve apostles. Thinking about these fellows, I can't help but marvel at all they laid aside to follow Jesus. They gave up everything to respond to Jesus's call to follow Him—careers, responsibilities, family, friends, even their lives.

I relate the most to Matthew, the former tax collector. I was an accountant for thirty-two years in my professional career. My title was controller. The irony in that title is not lost on me at all as the Lord has been leading me to give up control on so many things in this joyful journey of healing (body, mind, and spirit). It's easy to relate to where Matthew came from and appreciate his crazy career change.

I'm no longer balancing the accounting books because I recently quit my job (praise God). My life has changed drastically because I laid aside something tangible (a salary) for a faith-filled journey with Jesus—speaking, coaching, blogging, and writing books for Him. I don't think I'm going to miss balancing ledgers one bit.

In fact, I'm writing more than one book at this time. The one in your hands (now published) and one book about my joy-fueled healing journey with Jesus following a low-carb and fasting lifestyle, which will be ready for you to read soon. It's been a challenging season writing this second book. I've needed to process the emotions of overcoming a carb addiction while surrendering to being fully satisfied by the Word of God for my daily bread. I am learning to wait on the Lord for the full development of His message, a work in progress for the Lord.

Today, we see a short passage of Scripture in Luke 6:20–23 that could easily be the summary of my book as it relates to hunger and what satisfies the soul. Listen to Jesus share about joy. Looking at his disciples, he said:

> Blessed are you who are poor, for yours is the kingdom of God. *Blessed are you who hunger now, for you will be satisfied.* Blessed are you who weep now, for you will laugh. Blessed are you when people hate you, when they exclude you and insult you and reject your name as evil, because of the Son of Man. *Rejoice in that day and leap for joy*, because great is your reward in heaven. For that is how their ancestors treated the prophets." (vv. 20–23, emphasis mine)

There are days when I question the purpose of my calling to write and speak that God has placed over my life. Wouldn't it just be easier and faster to point people to Scripture and be done with it? I've struggled with thoughts like, "I'm not worthy. I'm not equipped. I'm not experienced. And people will hate me, exclude me, insult me, and reject me!" My former self would run and hide, but now I'm spurred on because of joy. My heart is leaping for joy, indeed.

Jesus regularly challenges us to do things that are hard, surprising requests to get us out of our comfort zone and grow us—like the challenges in this chapter. Love your enemies. Do not judge others. Bear good fruit. Build wisely.

Learning, trusting, and then actually *responding* is a process, wouldn't you agree? Let's go deeper into verses 20 and 21. Jesus isn't just talking about material poverty and physical hunger. Nope. He is speaking to us about our spiritual poverty and our hunger for righteousness. Two things we cannot disregard in our joy-seeking journey.

When we realize the full depth of Jesus's sermon here, we can respond to His encouragement to *rejoice and leap for joy*! Our reward for suffering and hardship will come one day, so we can set aside all the fear and worry of rejection to rise up and meet His challenges for us. Jesus satisfies every little and big need we have—physically, emotionally, and spiritually.

Hallelujah, Jesus had me at joy!

Today, let's join together as a body of believers and start building evidence of joy to reach this weary world in this Christmas season. Continue to daily dig deep into the richness of God's Word. Store up good things as you read and meditate on the gifts He's freely giving.

"For the mouth speaks what the heart is full of" (v. 45).

As you store and overflow with His joy, pray for Holy Spirit divine encounters to share this *good news of great joy!* As for me, in this new phase of my life, He overwhelms me every day with His goodness. He satisfies every craving of my soul. So, I'll keep speaking and writing words while following His lead.

Ponderings

Jesus makes some challenging requests in this chapter. What is He challenging you to do outside of your comfort zone in this Christmas season of joy?

Refer back to Luke 6 and find where Jesus speaks to the following: To do good or to do evil? To save life or to destroy it? If you love those who love you, what credit is that to you (it's too easy)? Can a blind man lead a blind man? Why do you look at the speck in your brother's eye and not the plank in your own? Why do you call me, "Lord, Lord," and do not do what I say? Contemplate these questions. Which one will you respond to today?

Finding Joy

Despite feeling uncomfortable in challenging situations, as we follow Christ and obey His words, He exhorts us to rejoice and leap for joy. We know for certain that there is a joy-filled celebration going on in heaven because of all the spiritual fruit on display for His glory.

Prayer

Heavenly Father, on the days I feel overwhelmed, isolated, rejected, and alone in this world, remind me that all of heaven is rejoicing when we serve You with our whole self: body, mind, and spirit. Help me to love those who persecute me. Prune me to bear good fruit for You so that everything I say and do overflows with joy to point everyone to You. Give me opportunities today, in this season of joy, to share the good news! Amen.

She brought a beautiful alabaster jar filled with expensive perfume. Then she knelt behind him at his feet weeping. Her tears fell on his feet, and she wiped them off with her hair. Then she kept kissing his feet and putting perfume on them.

Luke 7:37–38 NLT

JOY IN CHOOSING AN ALABASTER JAR

Can you name your absolutely most favorite Christmas gift you have ever received? I'm fifty-four years old, so I need a moment to think on this.

I see an interesting gift in the section about the sinful woman and an alabaster jar (vv. 36–50).

I've pondered the significance of this story for several years, ever since I heard the beautiful song "Alabaster" by my favorite band, Rend Collective. It's not one of their top hits, but it really ministers to my soul as I contemplate the heart of this story.

We learn from Luke that a sinful woman shows up at the home of a Pharisee with an alabaster jar of perfume. As Jesus was reclining in the home, the woman proceeds to cry and kiss His feet. Then she pours the perfume from her alabaster jar over His feet.

Picture the look on the face of the Pharisee. While he's standing there appalled, I wonder to myself, "Where does a prostitute get such an expensive alabaster jar of perfume?" and, "What would motivate her to spill such a treasure at the feet of Jesus?" Based on the little information we are given about these characters, I picture her as one of the "least of these" and the Pharisee as not lacking in any worldly thing.

So how would you answer my two questions above? I speculate that this alabaster jar is a gift from, ahem . . . a customer from her life of prostitution. That's just a wild guess. And it seems to me like this would be a cherished possession, a favorite gift?

Why would this woman choose this gift and this action to bring to the feet of Jesus?

Perhaps the jar is a physical reminder and representation of her sinful life. Maybe she had to get rid of it, sacrifice it therapeutically to heal her heart and find true joy and peace.

Furthermore, she's now living a life of humility and gratitude. She heard Jesus preach and made the life-changing decision to follow Him. The motivation was love. This act was evidence of her love and appreciation for the forgiveness of her sins. It was a second chance at a new life.

Unlike the Pharisee who offered Jesus nothing as a guest in his home (no water, no kiss, no oil—no offerings of gratitude), this woman chose a gift from the overflow of heartfelt joy. She likely chose the best material gift she'd ever received. It was something that cost her much by the world's standards, a priceless expression from a redeemed heart.

Jesus knew the depth of her love and confronted the appalled witnesses:

> "Therefore, I tell you, her many sins have been forgiven—as her great love has shown. But whoever has been forgiven little loves little." Then Jesus said to her, "Your sins are forgiven." The other guests began to say among themselves, "Who is this who even forgives sins?" Jesus said to the woman, "Your faith has saved you; go in peace." (vv. 47–50)

Indeed, I picture her leaving that scene rejoicing and leaping for joy!

All right, I've recalled a gift from my youth, which was one of my favorites. In the sixth grade I received an orange ten-speed bicycle. I loved the color orange, and I loved the freedom the bicycle gave me as I sped around the streets of my hometown with friends.

But I really had to put some thought to this question. Why? I'm sad to say it took fifty years before my passion for worldly possessions began to fade. And over the past several years, all this passion is now replaced with joy in the knowledge that Jesus is the best gift I ever received. And give.

It's almost a struggle now to find a gift of any value for family and friends. Does that make sense? Sometimes it leaves me at a loss for words.

That bicycle ended up buried in a scrap pile decades ago, no doubt. At the time it was a useful item, a prized possession, but in hindsight, it represents to me the worthlessness of everything I held in great importance for over five decades.

I'm a sinful woman but I strive, oh so hard, to present my joyful journey to Him with a great love. During particularly difficult days, I will sit at His feet and weep, especially during seasons of difficult hardships. If you're facing a Christmas season in the middle of hardships or if you're missing a loved one around your table, Jesus is inviting you to kneel at His feet and weep if you need to. He will dry your tears.

How can I be certain of this? He has dried my tears and constantly reminds me of the song of joy in my heart. Joy is a gift that leaves me eternally grateful. Jesus has asked me to give up so much by leaving the security of a stable income, but I have peace and joy.

The sinful woman chose joy in the alabaster jar. In return her story is a precious example to us all. I can think of no greater gift this Christmas season than to hear Him say, "Your faith has saved you; go in peace."

Pondering

As you think about gifts during this Christmas season, what cherished possession or daily practice is Jesus prompting you to sacrifice? What will it cost you?

As you make this difficult choice of sacrifice, where can you find the joy that Jesus wants you to experience in the surrender?

Finding Joy

Though it may cost you in worldly possessions, when you respond to Jesus from a heart overflowing with joy, He sees your sacrifice. He knows your heart and your faith and promises you peace in this Christmas season and beyond.

Prayer

Heavenly Father, please stir in me a true heart of sacrifice and surrender. Help me to be attentive to what You are calling me to do, whether it be to give up a cherished possession of this world or to courageously step into that uncomfortable space like the sinful woman who stepped into the Pharisee's home. I repent that I've been clinging tightly to the presents of this world, and instead, I surrender them at Your feet. Amen.

Today's Postscript:

Make sure you listen to the song I recommended—"Alabaster" by Rend Collective.

But the seed on good soil stands for those with a noble and good heart, who hear the word, retain it, and by persevering produce a crop.

Luke 8:15

SOWING JOY!

Joy jumps out to me today in between the hard places—like the rocks! In Luke 8:11–15 we read the well-known parable of the sower. If you recall, Jesus is teaching us how to sow a good crop for the kingdom of God. He's giving us an example of how spending time in God's Word makes for fertile ground, a soil conducive to exponential growth of joy and other fruits of the Holy Spirit. How will we respond?

By now it should be no secret to you what my motivation is for my daily writing to you. I'm passionate about you spending time in God's Word every day to develop your own personal passion with delight. Jesus drives this point home with His parable about sowing seed.

> This is the meaning of the parable: The seed is the word of God. Those along the path are the ones who hear, and then the devil comes and takes away the word from their hearts, so that they may not believe and be saved. Those on the rocky ground are the ones who receive the word with joy when they hear it, but they have no root. They believe for a while, but in the time of testing they fall away. The seed that fell among thorns stands for those who hear, but as they go on their way they are choked by life's worries, riches and pleasures, and they do not mature. But the seed on good soil stands for those with a noble and good heart, who hear the word, retain it, and by persevering produce a crop. (vv. 11–15)

Perhaps this year you've experienced some extremely difficult challenges. I understand difficult years. In recent years I've experienced enormous stress in what I call my "perfect storm." The storms included stress from events, such as a global pandemic, hormonal changes in my new stage in life (hello full-blown menopause and unwelcome health issues), and caring 24/7 for a loved one (totally unexpected circumstances considering all the hopes and dreams I have for this loved one—heartbreaking!). Oh, and my daughter got married and left the nest and I miss her terribly.

Truthfully, all of this has almost knocked me off my feet. Fortunately, quitting my corporate career has helped me manage some of the physical symptoms related to stress. It sounds like I have another book in me to share about how the Lord and God's Word sustained me through the storms. But for now, let's get back to the main lesson for today.

Reading verse 13 takes my breath away and gives me great pause. "Those on the rocky ground are the ones who receive the word with joy when they hear it, but they have no root. They believe for a while, but in the time of testing they fall away" (v. 13).

The rocky ground verse 13 describes is where I lingered, parched for decades. Every Christmas season I received the story with joy, but after a while it faded into the background. Christmas is all about joy. Like the Scripture says, it didn't take root. Joy never buried deep down in my soul. Just as Christmas comes and goes, there goes my fleeting joy.

But now my foundation has shifted, and I'm jumping for joy! I often tell people that God healed me for a reason in advance of the 2020 pandemic. His timing is perfect; if not for my daily delight in spending time in God's Word, a discipline I had developed early in my healing journey, that year would've done me in. I'm sure you can relate.

Friend, this is the best part of our healing story: spiritual transformation. It's a gift as a result of our dedication to and delight in spending time in God's Word every day. Just like Jesus says in verse 15—by reading, hearing, retaining, and persevering, anyone with a noble and good heart will produce a good crop for God's kingdom.

I'm so grateful that my seed is sown in good soil now. The fruit He wants to produce in us requires daily cultivating; daily time abiding in God's Word. It's my source of strength and joy and equips me, in my best effort, to produce good fruit. He gives each of us a story for His glory. Amen.

Don't sit on the side of the path. Don't trip over the rocks. And, don't allow the soil of your heart to become hardened so that the Word of God can't penetrate. Watch out for those thorns of life. Instead, dig into the richness of the soil of God's Word and watch Him restore, renew, and redeem your faith and your life. His Word is fertilizer and nourishment to sustain your walk in your God story.

Even the smallest seed of faith can generate great faith. That's all I had when I began crying out to God to heal my many afflictions. I have a great connection and appreciation for the sick woman in verses 42 through 48. This woman was plagued for years with a bleeding condition. What did she do? She dug deep down in her faith, and she reached out to touch the hem of His garment. By her faith she was instantly healed. Maybe she only had a tiny mustard seed of faith, but she was healed. Oh, what joy.

Like this woman, some days I have to grasp the hem of His garment. Are you holding tight too?

The Christmas story doesn't come and go like a winter season. The Christmas story lives forever. Join me in experiencing this unspeakable joy of the good news each and every day of the year.

Pondering

Where is God's Word sown in your life today? The side of the path? The rocky soil? Among the thorns? Or on fertile soil? What kind of crop are you producing for the kingdom? (Consider the fruits of the Spirit: love, joy, peace, patience, kindness, gentleness, faithfulness, goodness, and self-control).

What are you grasping on to for dear life today? Is it serving your story or God's story in you? Are you reading His Word daily?

Finding Joy

Deep and abiding joy is not fleeting. Joy is buried deep in the fertile soil of your heart and soul, overflowing when you obediently spend time in God's Word every day.

Prayer

Heavenly Father, thank you for the parable of the soil as a lesson to learn how deeply we must attend to and nuture our relationship with you. Help us not to take our relationship with You for granted by enjoying Your presence in our lives only occasionally. Give us a supernatural hunger and thirst for Your Word to develop a deeper and joy-filled, life-changing relationship with You. Amen.

Then he said to the crowd, "If any of you wants to be my follower, you must give up your own way, take up your cross daily, and follow me."

Luke 9:23 NLT

"FOLLOW ME" FOR JOY

My daughter is a thrill-seeking world traveler. The girl is only twenty-four years old and has already explored seven foreign countries and much of the United States.

In Zion National Park, she traversed a twisty trail on one of the most dangerous hikes at Angel's Landing. In Iceland's Thingvellir National Park, she suited up in a thermal suit for the icy waters and dove into the crack of two tectonic plates. On her South African honeymoon, with bungee cords strapped to her ankles, she jumped off Bloukrans Bridge, the highest commercial natural bungee jump in the world. Check out the video proof in the link provided in the *Seeking Joy* resources.

This begs the age-old question, "If your daughter jumped off a bridge, would you follow her?"

Absolutely not. As her mom, her adventures terrify me. She's begging me to visit some of these sites with her, but I am not a thrill-seeker.

I'm content with being a joy-seeker. That seems a lot safer, right? I'd be cool with taking pictures of her from behind the safety rails. One can never be too careful.

In Luke 9, we see an offer of adventure, one we should approach with great care. Jesus is dropping the ultimate thrill-seeking challenge in the crux of His gospel message.

"Then he said to them all: 'Whoever wants to be my disciple must deny themselves and take up their cross daily and *follow me*'" (v. 23, emphasis mine).

Follow me? I love to travel, though not to the level of excitement my daughter enjoys. So, I have to ask myself, am I willing to deny myself comfort in my travels? Am I willing to face my fears? If I devote my life to following Jesus, how will I pack? In verse three, Jesus tells His disciples to take nothing worldly for their journey. No staff, no bag, no bread, no money, no extra tunic. What? Talk about traveling light. Hmm.

In verses 57 through 62, Jesus outlines for us the cost of following Him. He has no place to lay His head, so it sure does sound like we will be on the move. Some men were interested in the journey, but as soon as He explained the high cost, they came up with their excuses. As Jesus considers their heart motivation (or lack thereof), He explains that we all must be ready and willing without looking back.

Jesus replied, "No one who puts his hand to the plow and looks back is fit for service in the kingdom of God" (v. 62).

So, no luggage and no looking back. This is a lot to consider.

My daughter and I have traveled together a lot. During my unhealthy years I never braved the fun things. Most of the time you would hear me making up an excuse to sit on the sideline or to wait in the car or at the bottom of the hill. I missed out on so much, and for that I am so sorry.

But I got better! Getting healthy for my kids and an active lifestyle was a big part of my motivation to succeed. My daughter is a nurse, so I didn't want to burden her with taking care of my sick self. (Besides, she'd probably be off traveling.)

During my thrilling weight loss journey, I discovered joy. And I also learned to trust Him for all my provisions. I stepped out into the unknown and it cost me a lot, but nothing compared to the joy I found in Jesus. Losing one hundred pounds is difficult and heart-wrenching work, and it required a lot of sacrifice and a heart of surrender to finally find success after decades of failures. But, again, in the process, I discovered joy and a deep affection for Jesus.

Friend, I don't want you to miss out on this joy ride with Jesus. Trust me, a journey of sanctification and striving to know Him deeper is a journey worth your time.

Are you scared? Like the excuses I give my daughter to avoid bungee jumping, you may feel paralyzed in fear considering the cost of following Jesus.

What if you traded your fear for finding joy in your journey today? Trust me, it is a thrill to stick with Jesus to see what adventure He has in store for you every day.

I love this quote from my marketing coach Patricia Durgin. "A disciple of Christ is following Him, being changed by Him, and committed to His mission for the world." How timely.

I will testify all day long that reading God's Word every day, choosing to follow Him, *will* change you. He *will* use you to change the world for His glory!

I love my daughter's passion for travel. She's quite frugal with money so she can go off regularly on more adventures. She's ready to jump on the next adventure at a moment's notice.

What if we apply the same traveling-light and trusting-Jesus-to-provide-for-us principles in a passionate pursuit to follow Jesus? I recently took this plunge with a tremendous leap of faith trusting He will provide for all of my needs when I sacrificed my corporate career salary to serve Him full time. Jesus might not be calling you to quit your job, but He is calling you to follow Him in the plan He has for your life.

Now I might be wrong, but I don't think Jesus will ask you to bungee jump off the Bloukrans Bridge today. But if He did, would you jump for joy? Make sure to take video for me.

Pondering

Just like Jesus expected the disciples to travel light, what is He asking you to leave behind today? What makes you nervous about following Him? What might this cost you?

Is the prospect for more joy appealing enough to lay aside what it will cost you? Are you ready to follow Him no matter the cost?

Finding Joy

Jesus is calling you into a joy-filled adventure with Him; be willing to delight in the sacrifice for His glory.

Prayer

Heavenly Father, teach me what it means to follow You. Show me the way. Help me to trust that You will meet my every need and You have more joy in store for me than I could possibly imagine. Let the excitement of this new adventure begin today in this Christmas season as I step out and share Your *good news of great joy* in this hurting world. Amen.

At that time Jesus, *full of joy* through the Holy Spirit, said, "I praise you, Father, Lord of heaven and earth, because you have hidden these things from the wise and learned, and revealed them to little children. Yes, Father, for this *is what you were pleased to do*. All things have been committed to me by my Father. No one knows who the Son is except the Father, and no one knows who the Father is except the Son and those to whom the Son chooses to reveal him."

Luke 10:21–22 (emphasis mine)

WITNESS AND WORSHIP WITH JOY

Martha, Martha, what shall we do with you? You are busy, busy, busy and seem a wee bit agitated. How can I help?

Ahh, Jesus is speaking to us all today, especially to us nurturing women during what for many of us is the most stressful and busy time of the year, am I right?

"'Martha, Martha,' the Lord answered, 'you are worried and upset about many things'" (v. 41).

Are you familiar with this story in verses 38 through 42? Martha is running about the home making preparations for a big day. Jesus is in her home. She's overwhelmed with busyness, perfecting the details, while her sister is enjoying the fun and festivities.

While Mary listened, Martha was distracted. I bet we can all relate to how overwhelmed Martha' feels in this scene, can't we?

Now, I've never claimed to be a Martha type, as I picture her preparing her home Martha Stewart style. Over the past few years, with the energy I've gained due to my healing journey, I am a bit tidier, and now at least willing to open my home for hospitality.

But I do claim being distracted most of the time, especially during these holiday months. In fact, as I strive to accomplish ministry work, some days I feel so distracted. I've asked over and over again for my praying partners to pray away distractions for me. I get what Martha is up against. Friend, in our tendencies towards perfection, we often lose our focus.

And then we complain. And maybe we come across as a "crabby patty," which my kids used to fondly call me. Yikes. It's true though. Distractions, to-do lists, and chronic health issues made me unpleasant to be around. We're supposed to be joyful during this season and create a special season for our family and kids, but it's hard to do when we are plagued by stress and the unrealistic expectations of perfection we set for ourselves.

Overwhelmed, Martha took her complaint to Jesus, and that's okay! I can't think of anyone better to take my complaints to as I trust that He will help me to sort them out. Just look how He helps Martha in this situation. "'Martha, Martha,' the Lord answered, 'you are worried and upset about many things, but few things are needed—or indeed only one. Mary has chosen what is better, and it will not be taken away from her'" (vv. 41–42).

Jesus loved Martha, and He was kindly calming her down and helping her to refocus on her first love. He's also offering her an alternative to choose what is better.

When I reflect back on my journey of transformation, I can see how Jesus constantly tried to gain my attention and shift my focus. During unpleasant days something serious separated me from satisfying all the things in my life. I filled the void with food and wasting time and money. I craved one thing, but I simply didn't know what I was missing to satisfy the longings of my soul.

Now I know. I never spent time daily in God's Word. Sure, I'd study and cram last minute for my lady's Bible study evenings. Cramming in thirty minutes before a session is not recommended.

I often felt so unworthy, and yet He chose to grab me and my life—my body, mind, and spirit. I struggle when I revisit my past, but as I read verses 21 and 22, I am so grateful knowing He chooses us.

At that time Jesus, *full of joy* through the Holy Spirit, said, "I praise you, Father, Lord of heaven and earth, because you have hidden these things from the wise and learned, *and revealed them to little children*. Yes, Father, for this is what you were pleased to do. All things have been committed to me by my Father. No one knows who the Son is except the Father, and no one knows who the Father is *except the Son and those to whom the Son chooses to reveal him.*" (vv. 21–22, emphasis mine)

Look at that. Jesus, *full of joy,* reminds us that He chose us. At some point in our journey, He reveals Himself to us. How will we respond?

I believe Mary's way is the best response, and it is Jesus approved. Like verse 39 says, she sat at the feet of Jesus and soaked it all in. This is something we should all do each and every day, especially during the Christmas season. For me, this is the daily, first-thing-in-the-morning practice of spending time worshipping God in His Word. With my coffee, of course, what I like to call my "Bible and beans" time. This has had the greatest impact on my joyful journey of healing. I cannot say this enough, and so forgive me if I will not shut up about it. Friend, your life *will* change when you choose to sit at His feet daily.

Choosing Jesus ushers in my renewed spiritual mindset and gives me the ability to always choose joy. Joy is contagious. Let this be our witness. Let us be true instruments of the joy of the Christmas season by worshipping every day at the feet of Jesus and spreading the *good news of great joy!*

Pondering

What is distracting you from choosing to sit at the feet of Jesus?

How will you respond to Jesus's invitation to choose what is better?

Finding Joy

Jesus chose you with a heart of joy. In response we can daily choose joy as we worship Him and witness for Him every day.

Prayer

Heavenly Father, help me when I am overwhelmed and distracted by things of this world. Remind me to be like Mary and to take the time to sit at Your feet and worship, especially during the busy time of the holidays. Thank You for choosing me as Your daughter. Be near me today as I choose to spread joy to everyone in this Christmas season and beyond. May they be overwhelmed by Your joy. Amen.

So I say to you: Ask and it will be given to you; seek and you will find; knock and the door will be opened to you. For everyone who asks receives; the one who seeks finds; and to the one who knocks, the door will be opened

Luke 11:9–10

GIVE GOOD GIFTS OF JOY

While my kids were growing up, I had a favorite Christmas tradition. Each year I would add a valuable Waterford crystal ornament to their collections. When money was tight, I planned and saved for these items.

My kids never *asked* for these on their wish lists; they weren't exactly thrilled over this Christmas line item on my budget. Nevertheless, the purchase was made each year. I love all things Irish, so these crystal ornaments make me smile. Also, I had a long-range plan with this collection of ornaments.

Today's chapter in Luke gives me great pause and regret for the former things I focused on—like making this annual Christmas purchase a priority, even when funds were short. If I could go back in time and apply the lessons Jesus is teaching us today in verses 11 through 13, I would in a heartbeat, because this section stopped my beating heart.

> "Which of you fathers, if your son asks for a fish, will give him a snake instead? Or if he asks for an egg, will give him a scorpion? *If you then, though you are evil, know how to give good gifts to your children, how much more will your Father in heaven give the Holy Spirit to those who ask him!*" (vv. 11–13, emphasis mine).

I think my plan of accumulating this collection of Waterford Christmas ornaments is a good gift. I had a long-range plan in mind when I began doing this, which came to fruition last December. I stored these gifts year after year with the intent to gift them to each child when they left our nest. As a newlywed, my daughter appreciated these sparkly ornaments for her first tree in her new home.

But hold up, my heart. My gift giving needed a rescue! What I didn't gift my kids with was a passion for the reason for the season. Yes, I took my kids to church during their early years. Yes, I dragged them to church during their early teen years. No, I couldn't wake them during their later teen years. Yes, now I *ask* them to come to church on Christmas and Easter with the incentive being it's the only gift I need (free, except for their time).

We rarely spoke about faith issues in our home. I don't recall reading the Christmas story in Luke to the kids. I counted on my church to do all this hard stuff. Sigh.

What's a momma to do with this? All I can do is take comfort in the lesson from Jesus today. Teach me Lord how to pray. "So I say to you: *Ask* and it will be given to you; *seek* and you will find; *knock* and the door will be opened to you. For everyone who asks receives; the one seeks finds; and to the one who knocks, the door will be opened" (vv. 9–10, emphasis mine).

Suppose you have children who don't prioritize their faith? Suppose you have loved ones and friends who make excuses and ignore the promptings of the Holy Spirit in their lives?

Jesus outlines the answers for us today in verses 2 through 4. *First,* we need to make sure our hearts are in alignment with His. "He said to them, 'When you pray, say: "Father, hallowed be your name, your kingdom come. Give us each day our daily bread. Forgive us our sins, for we also forgive everyone who sins against us. And lead us not into temptation."'"

Next, in the parable in verses 5 through 8, we learn we need to be persistent. The friend in search of bread for his one friend is driving his other friend crazy with his knocking, knocking, knocking on the door. I find descriptions of this behavior in two translations: shameless audacity (from the NIV) and impudence (from the ESV). Both can be summarized as a willingness to take bold risks.

This should embolden us to never give up on our loved ones. Jesus encourages us to ask, seek, and knock. These are three easy steps to memorize but three difficult steps to live out sometimes when we are not grounded in His Word.

I think I've found a solution to my question, "What's a momma to do?" As we continue our joy-seeking journey through this gospel message, let's strengthen our praying practices too.

Let's *ask* for our heart's desire: the joy of seeing our loved ones walking in faith.

Let's *seek* the wisdom and instruction we need: spending time daily in worship, seeking joy, and allowing that joy to overflow into the lives of our loved ones.

Let's *knock* continuously until those doors open: persisting in prayer, serving where needed, showering others with joy, and leading by example to the saving knowledge of grace.

Friend, in our shameless audacity, the Lord will answer our prayers and give the best gift of the Holy Spirit to those He loves.

Now, I have to admit, I think my gift of the valuable ornaments was creative and clever. But I'm sure you can guess that there is no comparison with the gift of Jesus born on that first Christmas morning.

A funny, not funny, memory just crossed my mind. I used to tell my kids when it came to Santa, "You have to believe to receive!" Oh my, how I emphasized the wrong message to receive.

So, thank You, Jesus, for the promise of the gift of the Holy Spirit and teaching us how to pray today. Doesn't His plan just overwhelm you and fill you with great joy that will be for all our precious loved ones?

Pondering

Take some time to reflect on the Lord's prayer in verses 2 through 4. How are you praising Jesus today? What are you trusting Him to provide? When is the last time you asked for His forgiveness? What temptations are you facing today?

Jesus reminds us to be bold and to ask, seek, and knock. Who do you need to be bold in praying salvation for today? How can you share joy with this person?

Finding Joy

Jesus shows us how to have a bold joy to share with others: ask, seek, and knock.

Prayer

Heavenly Father, thank You for this good gift of joy that I can boldly share with others. Help me to align my thoughts and my actions toward You to point others to the good gift of salvation that is waiting for them. Amen.

Then Jesus said to his disciples: "Therefore I tell you, do not worry about your life, what you will eat; or about your body, what you will wear. Life is more than food, and the body more than clothes."

Luke 12:22–23

KNOW JOY, NO WORRIES

In recent years we've witnessed pretty significant upheaval in our world. What's there to worry about? I saw your eyes roll. But seriously, our lists can get lengthy, right?

With all the uncertainty in the world, we do tend to worry. We worry about our children's education and future. Our spouse losing a job. The economy's impact on our business or retirement plans. The political climate. Health. Mental health. So many things weigh heavy on all of us right now.

I'll tell you something I've worried about. I knew Luke 12 included the section "do not worry" in verses 22 through 34, and I just knew the Holy Spirit would prompt me to write about a topic I'd rather avoid. This section of Luke shoots straight to my heart, and I'd rather say, "It's fine. I'm fine. Everything is fine!"

"Then Jesus said to his disciples: 'Therefore I tell you, *do not worry* about your life, what you will eat; or about your body, what you will wear. For life is more than *food,* and the body more than *clothes*'" (vv. 22–23, emphasis mine).

Ugh. He's talking about food. Awkward. Oh, and clothing. That pricks too.

I'll just blurt it out. For most of my life, I've been obsessed with food and designer labels.

Considering I checked off eight out of eight signs of food addiction, I admit I am a food addict.

Would you like examples of how I obsessed? Grabbing dessert first at the church potluck to make sure I enjoyed the best choice. Making sure I was first in line in a buffet. And hitting a fast-food drive through between mealtimes and hiding the evidence. Those are just a few examples—all signs pointing to three decades of deeply rooted heart issues.

You may not be obsessed with food or clothing, but maybe there is something in this material world creating worry in your head space. Something you don't trust God to provide. Can you say it out loud?

Jesus hears. He knows. Ravens don't prepare; they neither sow nor reap, and yet He assures us that He feeds them (v. 24).

Why do we worry so? I wish I had the magic answer to this question. Anxiety is at an all-time high these years. As Christ followers, we know better! Or at least we should know better. So why do we struggle so much?

Jesus knows: "If that is how God clothes the grass of the field, which is here today, and tomorrow is thrown into the fire, how much more will he clothe you—*you of little faith!*" (v. 28, emphasis mine).

The holidays are always hectic and busy, but does that justify our worry? Are you losing sleep at night as your thoughts race from little matters to great big matters? I invite you to sit in these verses and really pour it all out to Jesus; let Him put everything into proper perspective.

You are seeking joy through Luke for a purpose. God put you on this path, so you might as well embrace it. Do you need to increase your faith? Need hope? Not sure how to spread joy this Christmas season? I would like to assure you that you've taken the best first step in your faith. In fact, the time you spend in God's Word each day *will* grow your faith and increase your joy. It happened to me; it can happen to you. When I admitted I am a food addict, I actually meant that I am a recovering food addict. My recovery only began when I surrendered my struggles and my worries over to the Great Physician—Jesus. As I began my healing journey, I researched the Bible to find verses applicable to my struggles. The reference to food and clothing in verse 23 convicted my heart.

In my weak faith over the years of struggle, my thoughts solely focused on material possessions and food. I didn't trust Jesus with my food decisions, my food issues, or my weak faith. Not to mention, there was no joy in my heart.

But hallelujah! Jesus broke so many chains. My mindset is completely renewed to trust in Him for all my provisions. And my heart is full of unspeakable joy.

"And do not set your heart on what you will eat or drink; do not worry about it" (v. 29).

Friend, I pray these words of Jesus today will reset your heart and allow you to let go of that thing you're carrying. Jesus wants to carry these burdens for you—don't waste any more precious time. He has got you covered.

"But seek his kingdom, and these things will be given to you as well" (v. 31).

Trust me . . . there are lots of days I regret that I didn't seek the spiritual truth regarding my health issues. The day I figured it out I found freedom. And once you taste freedom, you will never go back into chains!

Let's make a pit stop on our journey; dump the worries on the side of the path, step out in faith, and jump for joy.

Pondering

Look up the definitions of worry and anxiety and write them here:

Which descriptions do you identify with? What worry or anxiety do you want Jesus to carry for you today?

Finding Joy

Jesus doesn't want us to worry about the overwhelming details of our life. Instead, He invites us to seek joy in relationship with Him. He will cover every need.

Prayer

Heavenly Father, help me to not live a life in fear, worry, or anxiety. I want to seek Your kingdom and treasure the joy in living Your promise for me. Today I lay down these worries that have consumed my thoughts. Grant me peace and joy to share today. Amen.

When Jesus saw her, he called her forward and said to her, "Woman, you are set free from your infirmity." Then he put his hands on her, and immediately she straightened up and praised God.

Luke 13:12–13

CULTIVATE JOY: PLANT AND GATHER

Every year, I like to choose a word after asking the Lord for His guidance. This word works something like a New Year's resolution—something to focus on and direct my journey with Him. During 2020, a year of isolation and staying at home, my word was actually "gather."

As 2020 dawned, I was so excited, planning the social gatherings in my mind with thoughts like these: "Oh yes, I am so excited about 2020 with all my plans to gather together with my writer and speaker friends at conferences—live and in person. And, oh yes, I'm so excited about gathering with my IF: Table sisters and my Jesus Girls. So many fun plans to gather together!"

Looking back, I could have considered the word "gather" a twisted prank. As we all know, there was to be no gathering with anyone, anywhere, anytime soon. Completely unbelievable. It left me questioning the Lord. Really, Lord? Gather?

My original social gathering thoughts on the word just touched the surface.

In Luke 13, Jesus shares with us the not so obvious lessons He wants us to learn about His application of the word "gather."

In several parables in Luke 13, we discover that even for Jesus, the process of gathering takes time and patience. This chapter emphasizes and encourages us to stick with the long journey; don't give up while waiting to see fruit.

Even Jesus yearned for so long to gather His beloved Jerusalem. "Jerusalem, Jerusalem, you who kill the prophets and stone those sent to you, how often I have longed to *gather* your children together, as a hen *gathers* her chicks under her wings, but you were not willing!" (v. 34, emphasis mine).

We know Jesus was on a mission and would not be derailed. He used the imagery of planting and producing food from plants in comparison to His kingdom in verses 18 through 21. We are called to help Jesus in the fields. How can we help Him in this gathering process?

This makes me think of the cultivation process, which is defined as fostering growth or improving by labor, care, or study.[4] It's definitely a time-consuming process. Cultivating joy, for example, takes time. There's a process: prune, plant, fertilize, nurture, produce, and then pick. I now see this is the big picture of the word God impressed on my heart, "gather." It's a journey.

A journey takes time, and often much longer than expected when we face opposition and obstacles. I didn't lose over one hundred pounds in quick fashion. You may not get out from under the burden of great debt this year. Your kids might not get back on track with school in the timetable in your mind. I know we want instant gratification—I know.

I'm sensing a theme of God's timing in this chapter as well. God is cultivating His perfect plan and, perhaps, not perfectly intent on gathering on our timetable. Look back in the parable of the yeast. I wonder if the woman with the leaven expected immediate results.

"Again he asked, 'What shall I compare the kingdom of God to? It is like yeast that a woman took and mixed into about sixty pounds of flour until it worked all through the dough'" (vv. 20–21).

That's a lot of dough permeated with a small amount of leaven. For me, the leaven is joy, which I cultivate daily by spending time in His Word—my daily bread. Eventually the joy expands and finally overflows. It affects my daily work and witness and gives me courage to plant seeds of His good news. Joy is contagious, like yeast—tiny granules of yeast. It's an honor to spread this contagion and watch Jesus gather His followers.

Jesus might gather us when we least expect Him to. Just like the crippled woman in the synagogue on the Sabbath. There is no mention of her speaking to Jesus in verses 10 through 17. I love that Jesus sees her, heals her, and sets her free from her years of infirmities.

"When Jesus saw her, he called her forward and said to her, 'Woman, you are set free from your infirmity.' Then he put his hands on her, and immediately she straightened up and praised God" (vv. 12–13).

He sees her. He sought her out. This fills my heart with so much joy.

After decades of ill health, I resigned myself to poor health for life. But at my weakest, I summoned a mustard seed of faith and begged God to heal me. I felt so unseen for so many years that I didn't think He'd answer. But I told Him I just wanted to feel better.

Words are inadequate to express the healing He provided to my whole self. I only anticipated physical healing; and I'm so humbled by the emotional and spiritual journey He also guided me through. This healing has led to unexpected excitement and joy in my new full-time job for Jesus.

What do you think about asking the Lord for a word of the year for you? I love this practice when we lean in and open our hearts to the jaunts in the journey of understanding what He is teaching us. Sometimes it takes us a full year to figure out the purpose, but that's okay. Cultivating takes time.

Pondering

If you are interested in finding a word of the year, ask the Holy Spirit to guide you in this decision. Write a short prayer of anything God is impressing on your heart right now.

As you reflect on this year, if you had a word of the year, has the significance of your word changed? If you didn't have a word for this year, is there a word that would summarize your journey with Jesus?

Finding Joy

We see Jesus longing to gather Jerusalem in verse 34, but they were unwilling. There is great and contagious joy when we allow Jesus to gather us and grow our faith.

Prayer

Heavenly Father, create in me an open heart with eyes to see and ears to hear the work You have for me to do. Keep me in Your Word daily, Lord, so that Your truth is planted deep in my inner being. Cultivate my life, Lord. Prune me where needed. Help me to grow in wisdom, knowledge, and joy so I can share the good news with everyone. Amen!

And whoever does not carry their cross and follow me cannot be my disciple.

Luke 14:27

Joy and Delight in the Sacrifice

I have a love-hate relationship with excuses. Some days I love them when my to-do list remains unfinished. Other days I want to kick myself when I've allowed them to overrule my resiliency.

Recently my excuses kept me from exercising, which should be an important part of my healthy lifestyle. I'm frustrated because I used to exercise daily. But then came the excuses.

My shoulder ached and eventually burned with every movement. I finally went to the doctor and received the diagnosis of a torn rotator cuff, bicep tendonitis, bursitis, and bone edema. While I healed, I backed off on the strain of exercise for my entire body. Hello, lower body? I slacked off there, as well.

As my shoulder healed, I launched into full-blown menopause with horrendous hot flashes and night sweats. Who wants to pump up the heat in that situation? Not me! I love my valid excuses. Can you relate?

What do I hate about excuses? Well, first they bring on a sense of shame over my failures. And on top of that, I feel responsible for motivating people to achieve their own results in their joyful journey to whole and healthy living. I've been known to lovingly remind people, "Hey, you've derailed. Stop making excuses!" They probably secretly hate that.

I appreciate the timing of this chapter because in just the past few days, it's helped me to stop making excuses to exercise. Let's see what Jesus says about our notorious excuse-making today.

> When one of those at the table with him heard this, he said to Jesus, "Blessed is the man who will eat at the feast in the kingdom of God." Jesus replied: "A certain man was preparing a great banquet and invited many guests. At the time of the banquet he sent his servant to tell those who had been invited, 'Come, for everything is now ready.' But they all alike began to make *excuses*." (vv. 15–18, emphasis mine)

In this parable of the great banquet, Jesus is inviting a chosen group of people to come and sit at His table. For whatever reason, these people reject the invitation and come up with disingenuous excuses.

Well, He wants to fill His table. Now what?

> The servant came back and reported this to his master. Then the owner of the house became angry and ordered his servant, "Go out quickly into the streets and alleys of the town and bring in the poor, the crippled, the blind and the lame." (v. 21)

He's just opened the invitation up to the least of these. Those who turned down His original invite will be shocked. "I tell you, not one of those men who were invited will get a taste of my banquet" (v. 24).

Choosing not to accept this seat at the Master's table brings a disastrous result. It is excuse-making for the ultimate demise.

I don't know about you, but I don't want to land on the "uninvited" list. What's the price for readmission?

This brings me back to my excuses. For decades I excelled at seeking and finding reasons to defend or justify my poor health. I tried so many man-made diet solutions over and over again. "Nothing works" was my best excuse.

Now with my shoulder healed and hot flashes controlled, my typical excuse for neglecting exercise is lack of time. We are all good at convincing ourselves there's no time, but we all have twenty-four hours in a day, seven days a week. I've convinced myself there's no time. What a wake-up call! Pun intended.

How did I get myself back on track? One word, and it is cringe worthy.

Sacrifice.

I hate thinking about sacrificing anything when struggling in my big, hairy messes.

Do you hate it too? It's going to cost you. In fact, in verses 25 through 33, Jesus is calling us to give up everything. Everything? Yep. It's time to pick up our cross, friend.

"And whoever does not carry their cross and follow me cannot be my disciple" (v. 27).

To pick up, you need to put down. What will you sacrifice today?

I consider the first step I took in my healing journey a huge sacrifice. On March 10, 2016, I quit sugar! Who knew just a few short years later my journey would be full of joy, and my life would be changed from one (seemingly) small sacrifice?

In hindsight I know that sugar symbolized a great big idol in my life. Do you have an idol? Is it money? A drive for success? Beauty? Gossip? Pride?

What if you put it down and pick up your cross? I have an idea your life will change drastically. Of course, my journey is still a work in progress. I mean, I did just fess up that I'm still prone to make excuses regarding exercise (among other things). We would be wise to take these words of Jesus seriously: "In the same way, those of you who do not give up everything you have cannot be my disciples" (v. 33).

This chapter convicts me—body, mind, and spirit. Consider the excess of time the Lord gives us when we have our priorities straight. As I continue on the joy-seeking journey, my mindset moved through these steps:

- Subtract excuses.
- Add surrender.
- Add sacrifice.
- Add sanctification.
- Add saving grace.

This all equals joy.

Now isn't that a delightful and worthy sacrifice? What better timing in the middle of the Christmas season? Even if you're in the midst of hardships or deep sorrows, don't miss this opportunity, friend.

My pastor, Adam Groh, posed the perfect question in a sermon.[5] "The Lord is asking, 'Take everything away, will you now worship my Son?'"

He's inviting you to the great banquet table. It's guaranteed to be the most joyful celebration you've ever experienced. Will you take seat?

Pondering

In verses 28 through 32, we find examples of people counting the cost to follow Christ—through reconciling a budget and negotiation in their equation. What comes to your mind as you consider the cost of following Christ?

What are you putting down to pick up the cross? As you reconcile this in your mind, identify the pros and cons. Will you follow?

Finding Joy

The idea that Jesus is inviting us personally to His great banquet table should fill our hearts with unspeakable joy. The sanctification journey will fill your life with this joy.

Prayer

Heavenly Father, I praise Your name that You have chosen me as a child of Your kingdom. Help me walk my journey on this earth with joy in my heart as You guide me on the path of surrender and sacrifice for Your glory. I leave all my excuses at the foot of Your cross and pick up my own cross today. Let my obedience be a witness to those who are spending time counting the costs. Speak to them in this Christmas season so that they can join me in this sanctification journey. Amen.

Then Jesus told them this parable: "Suppose one of you has a hundred sheep and loses one of them. Doesn't he leave the ninety-nine in the open country and go after the lost sheep until he finds it? And when he finds it, he *joyfully* puts it on his shoulders and goes home. Then he calls his friends and neighbors together and says, '*Rejoice* with me; I have found my lost sheep.' I tell you that in the same way there will be more *rejoicing* in heaven over one sinner who repents than over ninety-nine righteous persons who do not need to repent."

Luke 15:3–7 (emphasis mine)

FOUND IN JOY!

Today is my son's birthday. He was due on Christmas day. Imagine the wonder and awe as we anticipated the arrival of our first child. He graciously made his appearance into our lives ten days early, such an early Christmas blessing, indeed. The past few years in my Luke journeys, reading these parables about the lost and found, including one about a son, gives me so much to ponder.

I lost my son once when he was about four years old. I physically lost him in a crowded baseball stadium.

It happened in an instant, a moment of distraction. While at the concession stand, I took my eyes off of him to pay the cashier. I suppose I trusted him to stick by my side, but his curiosity got the best of him. He wandered off when the crowd went crazy for a home run. Distractions led him away from safety as he followed the excitement of the cheering crowd.

The good news? Although time seemingly stopped, I found him within a few minutes. He probably doesn't recall, but he received the tightest squeeze that day. Praise the Lord!

Fast forward twenty-plus years. My son and I have been on an unexpected journey the past few years. Someday I'll be able to share more with you (there's a book in my brain), but for now, I'm walking alongside him and loving on him through this journey. And this momma's heart is praying, praying, praying.

Our journey has been confusing, frustrating, and isolating. I know the enemy is trying to steal our joy; the battle rages on every day. But when you mess with my kid, I armor up—trust me.

What's a momma to do about these overwhelming feelings? I feel lost in the uncontrollable situation. There are many days my mind wanders and I'm prone to fret and worry over his health—physically, emotionally, and spiritually. But then I remember the real stories Jesus shares about the lost in Luke 15.

"Then Jesus told them this parable: 'Suppose one of you has a hundred sheep and loses one of them'" (vv. 3–4).

One lost sheep out of one hundred? Seems hopeless and a burden to find one lost sheep. Many days a sense of hopelessness penetrates me through cracks created by weariness. Of course, I had many hopes and dreams for my son on the day he was born. I would move heaven and earth to find my lost son.

Jesus feels the same way about us.

> Doesn't he leave the ninety-nine in the open country and go after the lost sheep until he finds it? And when he finds it, he *joyfully* puts it on his shoulders and goes home. Then he calls his friends and neighbors together and says, "*Rejoice* with me; I have found my lost sheep." I tell you that in the same way there will be more *rejoicing* in heaven over one sinner who repents than over ninety-nine righteous persons who do not need to repent. (vv. 4–7, emphasis mine)

More rejoicing in heaven than the moment I found Kyle when he was lost in the crowd? Right now, I'm picturing Jesus carrying Kyle on His shoulders, which releases the weight off of mine. Such a relief.

This unexpected experience with my son is teaching me an important lesson. When I find myself fretting and worrying over the future, I must trust that Jesus loves my son beyond my ability and beyond my wildest imagination. Jesus planned out Kyle's life for a purpose, and I know He is in control over his whole health.

I'm positive my joyful journey improved my emotional health just in time to face this storm in our lives. I shudder to think where I would be as the emotionally immature person I used to be. I envision myself stuck in my bed with the covers pulled over my head, avoiding the messy and the hard. Running to God's Word first thing every day keeps me sane.

Run to the Word. I like that. Now think about a loved one's circumstance that would prompt you to run.

Who just crossed your mind? Indeed, we all have loved ones who need healing and salvation. Jesus loves your son, daughter, husband, mom, dad, and all your loved ones—unfathomably.

In this chapter Jesus repeats the lesson on "lost and found" in three different parables: the lost sheep, the lost coin, and the lost son. I wonder, "Does He think we don't get it?" A total possibility. But then I remembered the importance of the number three. Biblically, the number three represents harmony, new life, and completeness.

Does He reiterate this truth three times to remind us that His plan will be fulfilled to completion for our loved ones? Because, friend, I know how much we fret and worry. I'm going to choose to find comfort and joy in this gift of new life for the lost. I think we should fatten the calf and plan a huge celebration. Oh, what a day of rejoicing that will be!

I rejoice since I can celebrate Kyle's birthday with him—here in our home. It gives me a sense of hope—he won't be lost again if I have any control, which I don't. But Jesus does. Hallelujah.

Pondering

Are you feeling lost in a difficult circumstance? Or are you weary in your prayers for a prodigal son (daughter, etc.)? What does Jesus promise you in today's Scripture?

Think of three characteristics of Jesus from these parables that will give you hope and comfort.

Finding Joy

Jesus's heart overflows with joy for you. So much so, he'll risk leaving the ninety-nine to lead you safely home. Rejoice in His heart for you.

Prayer

Heavenly Father, I am amazed by Your love. You care so much for the one sinner that You seek that sinner out with a passion to restore their joy. Thank You for the times when that sinner is me. I rejoice greatly in our reunion. I pray for this same joyful celebration for my lost loved ones. Let this Christmas season be the time for them to be found. Amen.

He said to them, "You are the ones who justify yourselves in the eyes of men, but God knows your hearts."

Luke 16:15

THE HEART OF JOY

My jaw dropped as I read this text message from my daughter.

"Mom, a really upset lady at the counter just threw all her change at me and it went all over the floor."

What in the world? Welcome to the life of working with the public, kiddo. Her trial by fire happened at *our local hometown* carry-out pizza joint during her training to wait on customers. Kaitlin is a math whiz and as smart as they come in solving messy problems. Counting money is a no-brainer. But the one thing she hadn't been trained on yet was how to open the closed cash drawer after a sale.

Apparently, this lady wanted to add extra coins to the transaction to receive back paper bills. With the drawer shut, the trouble began.

Now, I know my daughter. She doesn't get flustered easily and she doesn't have a rude bone in her body. This lady simply ran out of patience with a teenage new employee in a store.

So, she threw a handful of change at her. Yikes.

I also know my daughter well enough to feel her embarrassment. And my heart broke for her in that moment.

I used to be that lady. Well, no, I never threw a handful of coins at a kid (what a relief). But the thought may have crossed my mind. "If you don't know how to count back change, you should go back to school." Right? I used to be a chronic eye-roller and heavy sigher. I'm cracking myself up right now as I practice my eye-rolling and sighing again for old times' sake.

Truly, there's nothing funny about my prior behavior. Today my joy-seeking heart lands on one verse I never want to overlook again, Luke 16:15.

"He said to them, 'You are the ones who justify yourselves in the eyes of men, *but God knows your hearts*. What is highly valued among men is detestable in God's sight'" (v. 15, emphasis mine).

First off, I always valued money over many things in my life. I'm positive my focus on finances was heartbreaking to the Lord. I always felt a twinge of heavy guilt when I would read verse 13: "No servant can serve two masters. Either he will hate the one and love the other or he will be devoted to the one and despise the other. You cannot serve both God and Money" (v. 13).

It took several years, but I'm grateful that Jesus opened my eyes to the truth in this Scripture and prompted me to finally leave my corporate job and completely trust Him. There is so much joy and excitement in this newfound freedom in working exclusively for Him.

Another not-so-funny confession for you. A friend from my past and I used to ask each other, "Why can't everyone be perfect like us?" Whoa. I always chuckled it off as a joke. The truth? It revealed the state of my heart—dark.

The Pharisees who loved money sneered while being schooled by Jesus (verse 14). I get that. Ridiculing people came easily. Mostly in my mind and thoughts, but often lashing out at people in public. They needed a piece of my mind. Sigh.

I'm pondering the last part of verse 15 . . . "What is highly valued among men is detestable in God's sight."

What in the world did I value so highly to drive that behavior? Perfection. Stubbornness. Lack of compassion. Self-centeredness. I can go on, but you get the idea.

Did you learn the song *Joy Down in My Heart* as a child?

I've got the joy, joy, joy, joy down in my heart.
Down in my heart.
Down in my heart.
I've got the joy, joy, joy, joy down in my heart.
Down in my heart to stay.[6]

Guess what? It didn't stay for me. As I've walked the steps in solving my big, hairy mess, I know exactly why.

I never spent regular time in the Word of God. I probably picked up my Bible about twenty-six times each year to prepare for my bi-weekly Bible study. And that's a high estimate because sometimes I neglected to pick it up and skipped Bible study altogether.

Here in Luke 16, Jesus is warning us of the things of this world that separate us from Him. Our only assurance for keeping that *joy, joy, joy, joy down in our heart* is to run away from the darkness and head straight toward the light.

"The master commended the dishonest manager because he had acted shrewdly. For the people of this world are more shrewd in dealing with their own kind than are *the people of the light*" (v. 8, emphasis mine).

I desire to be among the people of light. Wise and shrewd in the gifts He's given me to help others. Thank you, Jesus, for giving me a heart of joy, teaching me how to handle the worldly riches You bestow and shining a light on the path of my joyful journey.

I highlighted the mention of *our local hometown* above for two reasons. First, I regret and apologize to anyone in, around, near, or nowhere near my hometown if you were a victim of my short-tempered behavior. I've got joy to share with you now.

Second, as a reminder to take this lesson to heart. My daughter's experiences in working with the public in her hometown soured her love for this hometown. As a result she refused to buy a house here. Yeah, yeah, I told her she will find this behavior in any old town . . . but perhaps having coins thrown in your face just stings.

Let's *be* the *change* and share a heart of joy this Christmas season and every season, bubbling up and over from down in our hearts to stay!

Pondering

During the hustle and bustle of the Christmas season, think of a time when your patience wore thin or your pride caused you to treat someone poorly. What warnings from Jesus do you take away from chapter 16?

Spreading joy takes practice. Can you recall a recent situation when you chose to share joy rather than lose your temper? What can you do to practice this daily, especially during the Christmas season?

Finding Joy

Jesus models how to spread joy instead of judgment in our interaction with the world.

Prayer

Heavenly Father, thank You for these lessons today teaching me how to act in my daily affairs and treatment of others. Help me to remember that the work You've called me to is about You. Remove my pride. Let Your joy shine bright in this Christmas season for the world to see that You are the Way, the Truth, and the Light of this world. Amen.

The apostles said to the Lord, "Increase our faith!"

Luke 17:5

INCREASE YOUR JOY

"The weary world rejoices."

This is the message that had been playing over and over in my mind—God's message to me amidst my complaints to Him over my weariness of a particularly stressful year. I sensed the Lord was prompting me to expand my Luke Christmas Countdown blog series and I almost refused to obey Him.

I reasoned that you, yes you, friend, would just be able to find this advent countdown through Luke on my old blogs. "It's there, Lord." And He kept singing in my ear, "The weary world rejoices, the weary world rejoices." I agree. I'm weary, we are all weary. And then the Holy Spirit flipped the light switch and I finally realized He was emphasizing the word *rejoice,* not weary. He was nudging me to share about *joy* because I know a few things about seeking it. So, here we are on this journey (thank you again for joining me).

Given my state of weariness at the time, I know I had the faith, but I needed desperate help from Him. Of course Jesus shows up with encouragement today in chapter 17.

"He replied, 'If you have *faith* as small as a mustard seed, you can say to this mulberry tree, "Be uprooted and planted in the sea," and it will obey you'" (v. 6, emphasis mine).

I jumped in full of faith, but I knew I better ask for some support. I asked my speaking and writing community to pray for me (they would understand). One of my speaking mentors Lori Boruff commented one word on my post: *Increase!*

This one word she shared sparked so much joy for this journey writing through Luke. What a coincidence she used *increase*. I had just witnessed a huge increase in the number of visitors on my old Luke Christmas Countdown blog post on December 1. The daily visitors on my website spiked from a few hundred visitors average to 3,500 visitors that day. And they all landed on my Luke Countdown. (Go God!) I didn't promote this old blog anywhere. How is this possible for my little lifestyle blog?

I went to my source for answering these types of questions. Dr. Google provided the statistics. If you Google "Christmas Countdown Luke," my old blog post appears as the number one hit of seven million. Seven million! Holy moly, I've never been a number one Google hit before. *Increase*, indeed. I started pondering this word as my word in the upcoming year.

Just for fun I went to the Dayspring online quiz to see what it would generate for me. All right, I don't count on a website application to determine my word of the year, but it's still fun to see how things line up.

My Dayspring word: *Connect*.

Hmm. Not increase, but my mind started spinning.

How can there be increase if you don't connect? Holy wow. You cannot. Do you see the confirmation and connection, I do? So exciting.

That's not all. Of course, we find the concept of *increase* right here in chapter 17. AH-mazing!

As I claimed this word *increase*, I desired to understand what the Lord would reveal. I'm asking Him for this gift, just like the disciples did in today's passage:

The apostles said to the Lord, *"Increase our faith!"* (v. 5, emphasis mine).

These guys travel with Jesus every day, why do they need their faith increased?

Because Jesus just shared a sticky lesson with them about rebuking sin and offenses in the body of Christ. I'm a big fan of "re" words, except rebuke. Ouch.

In my spiritual immaturity, I would run away from the scenario Jesus describes in verses 1 through 4; having to confront people for their sins and offenses, I'd rather not. Conflict makes me squirm, likewise the disciples. Even they dreaded conflict and asked for a greater measure of faith. An increase!

Unfortunately, I had to implement this Jesus lesson recently. As I came back to chapter 17, I discovered notes in the margin over a difficult situation this year. I prayed, "Lord, increase my faith." For the first time in my life, He filled me with a boldness. I attribute this boldness to the increase in faith, hope, and joy through reading His Word daily.

I shared about my former short-tempered self. The healing from this continues into this section on sin, faith, and duty to Christ (vv. 1–10). To be clear, for the first time in my life, I confronted offenses in love. Wow. I didn't lose sleep. I didn't drag others along on the gossip train. I didn't bad mouth the person. I didn't cuss them out. I didn't walk into the room with the attitude of Mrs. Always Right.

And it was so freeing. I testify my joy increased in confrontation. Crazy, I know! I went all in with a heart set on forgiveness, because that's what Jesus commands. As we focus on joy through another Christmas season, wouldn't this be an appropriate time to increase and share the grace and forgiveness which Jesus was born to share?

Surviving a situation over conflict brings a new perspective on the duty Jesus explains here:

"So you also, when you have done everything you were told to do, should say, 'We are unworthy servants; we have only done our duty'" (v. 10).

With the proper attitude, we won't seek recognition. We might be completely in the right, but we don't have to let that derail the process of reconciliation. We simply do everything through our calling to serve the Master. If that means rebuke, then you better be prepared. It won't hurt so much. Trust me.

Friend, I encourage you to pray for increase. Pray for it in every single fruit of the Spirit: love, joy, peace, patience, kindness, goodness, faithfulness, gentleness, and self-control (Galatians 5:22–23). Imagine how this looks in your personal situation. Christmas is a season filled with extra joy and peace. Let's not spend another Christmas season angry or upset with someone in our lives. Pray for God to increase your faith and boldness and give the best gift of all in this Christmas season—the gifts that Jesus freely gives us.

When we approach sticky situations with such *increase,* the peaceful resolution will bring Jesus the glory. And who knows, maybe you'll end up *connecting* with a new best friend.

Pondering

Christmas often prompts us to pause and contemplate difficult family situations. Recall a sticky situation which ended even stickier because of the way you handled it in your human nature. What went wrong?

What could you pray for the Lord to increase to handle these types of situations with joy in your heart?

Finding Joy

Jesus reminds us today if we have faith and we ask, we can increase our joy.

Prayer

Heavenly Father, You are the giver of all good things in our life. As we focus on gifts this Christmas, help me to remember to ask for increase and praise You for the gifts of love, joy, peace, patience, kindness, goodness, faithfulness, gentleness, and self-control. Help me use these gifts when facing confrontation with other believers so that we can both walk away from the situation in love and with forgiveness. Amen.

Then Jesus told his disciples a parable to show them that they should always pray and not give up.

Luke 18:1

PERSISTENT JOY

I wrote this from a medical office lobby today. My son was being tested, yet again. This arduous journey wears on us all. But as the best advocate for my son, I will not relent in seeking answers for his best care. Insurance giants would prefer we give up . . . never. Many hopeless days my son wants to give up. What's a mom to do? I'm seeking joy in today's reading for answers.

Right away, Luke gives away the major theme of Luke 18 in the first verse: "Then Jesus told his disciples a parable to show them that they should always pray and not give up" (v. 1).

Yes, that's the reminder I needed on this day. We could stop our reading right there, but the subtitle of this section in my NIV Study Bible, "The Persistent Widow," begs us to continue. The key words in this verse are "not give up," in other words *persistence.* Let's keep going.

Kyle mentioned he slept horribly last night. Same here. Sliding out of bed, I begged God to be with us for the day. Sure enough, He met me right in His Word in chapter 18 in these parables and stories. Another mind-blowing God-incident.

From the persistent widow seeking justice in verses 1 through 8 all the way through to the blind beggar receiving his sight in verses 35 through 43, we find the encouragement to persist; to never give up. *Always pray and do not give up.*

I also see resiliency. As I scroll social media and speak to friends in heartache, I'm certain we all need an extra dose of resiliency right now. Unfortunately, Christmastime may be difficult for many, but add on overwhelming world events . . . yeah, it makes us weary. Sigh. No wonder so many are giving up hope, giving up their joy. Resigning to isolation, worrying over their health, and sadly, dealing with the loss of loved ones to a virus and other illnesses. Others face job loss and financial stress. Yes, Lord. The world is weary. How do we retain our Christmas peace and joy?

Facing the general public today is a challenge. So many opinions. In frustration, people's tempers are short (in any season, actually). Those with the loudest voices will rebuke us in an attempt to shut down our faith and steal our joy. The devil is busy creating chaos with the intent to separate us from our Savior, imploring us to be quiet.

That's a real challenge for us, but look who the disciples are rebuking in this chapter—those trying to get their children in front of Jesus and a blind beggar. The least of these in the disciples' eyes. I found this rather confusing but let's persist to figure this out.

> People were also bringing babies to Jesus to have him touch them. When the disciples saw this, they *rebuked* them. But Jesus called the children to him and said, "Let the little children come to me, and *do not hinder them,* for the kingdom of God belongs to such as these. I tell you the truth, anyone who will not receive the kingdom of God like a little child will never enter it." (vv. 15–17, emphasis mine)

The word *hinder* pops out—something which gets in the way of persistence. While Jesus rebukes the disciples, "Do not hinder them," there is hope for the world and our difficult storms. Children trust so easily, is it possible to trust God so easily? Is something hindering your trust?

Never in a million years would I expect to be dragging my son to so many doctor appointments. I lament over his injury and am prone to ask why. I catch myself slipping into brief moments of dread and hopelessness over our situation. Well, I don't actually catch myself, but the Holy Spirit rebukes me and comforts me in these moments. And look, this day, on an important day in our journey, He gave me the story of a persistent woman and a beggar. I'm a woman—more precisely a momma bear. I'm a beggar, begging for a sign of hope and most importantly to retain my joy.

Let's check out the rest of the story on the blind beggar in verses 35 through 43. I'm in awe over this street scene.

Sitting in his blindness, hopelessness probably overwhelmed him. There was nothing he could do to improve his lot in life.

As he heard the crowd approaching, I'm struck by his first plea for mercy. Despite his blindness, he believed in the Messiah.

"He called out, 'Jesus, Son of David, have mercy on me!'" (v. 38).

After that cry, he got the smackdown from the disciples. Yikes. How blind were these disciples to what was about to go down?

But not to be deterred, the beggar cried out again.

Those who led the way rebuked him and told him to be quiet, but he shouted all the more, "Son of David, have mercy on me!" (v. 39).

I'm cheering now for the boldness of the blind beggar. How about you? The world tried to shut him up, but his faith would not remain silent.

He captured the attention of Jesus because of his persistence. Jesus restored his sight. Hallelujah—such a tremendous blessing.

The whole scene ends with the beggar following Jesus and dancing in the streets with joy. And guess what? The whole crowd rejoiced as they experienced this contagious joy.

While you face your trials today, first of all remember He sees you. He loves you. Then continue to cling to the reminders here from Jesus. Be persistent in your joy-seeking journey. Pray without ceasing and do not give up.

I am still walking this journey with my son, but I trust in God for answers soon for the best care for my son. Through this Scripture today, I know that if God has more difficulties in store in this journey, I shall persist with joy. Guaranteed.

Pondering

Your only hope for a cure from your blindness is Jesus. Do you believe this truth?

What practical application from your joy-seeking journey can you put into play to increase your boldness in persistently seeking answers from God? How can you use the Christmas season to make a greater impact on the weary world around you?

Finding Joy

With a strong faith, don't ever give up on the blessings and gifts God has in store for you. Your persistence will pay off, leaving you dancing in the streets with joy.

Prayer

Heavenly Father, even in my weariness and overwhelming circumstances, thank You for the ways You encourage me and remind me to always pray and never give up. Keep me in Your Word and present in persistent prayers each day. I trust You to turn my overwhelming situations into awe in Your overwhelming love. My heart overflows with joy when You meet me in these places. Thank you for this gift of joy and your love this Christmas season. Amen.

And when Jesus came to the place, he looked up and said to him, "Zacchaeus, hurry and come down, for I must stay at your house today." So he hurried and came down and received him joyfully.

Luke 19:5–6 ESV

December 19—Luke 19

FEELING LOST?
SEEK JOY!

Over the years I've learned valuable financial lessons over the provisions the Lord bestows. Early in my adult years, I carried a heavy burden of credit card debt. Only, I didn't acknowledge the weightiness of this burden. My blasé approach created a vicious cycle of spend and pay down, spend and pay down. Oh boy, just like my yo-yo dieting!

Now you would think as a career accountant I would know better. Hey, hey, that's what zero percent credit card offers are for, right? Being sucked into living in a material world filled many cravings—wanting for something more. But what?

Maybe the wealthy tax collector, Zacchaeus, relates? Today we witness him living the good life, comfortable in his worldly riches.

We see in verses 1 through 10, just like me, there's something deep in Zacchaeus's soul prompting him to seek something different, something better. God stirred something in his heart soon to be fully realized.

Stirred up enough to climb a tree! What?!? Small statured myself, I know crowds are problematic. Zacchaeus took extreme action. You won't catch me climbing trees. Praise God the Holy Spirit nudges with alternatives to sneak a peek.

Whatever prompted Zacchaeus to take that first step, I don't know. But watch this: Jesus *looked up*! In a huge crowd, Jesus noticed the lost and seeking Zacchaeus.

Somehow God grabbed my attention when it came to my financial resources, and the weight of debt no longer weighs me down. But

I missed the big lesson in that season because I still shopped for sense-less things and still didn't develop a joy-filled relationship with Jesus.

What finally grabbed my attention? My health issues. My joy meter registered zero. I even lost my joy for singing and quit the worship team. Instead, I lived with mounting chronic health issues and a broken heart. Enough to bring me to the feet of Jesus to cry for mercy and healing. Behold, my climbing tree.

Until then I lived and breathed for self. Comforts of keeping up with the Joneses, comforts of making my own decisions, comforts of living safe in my upper middle-class neighborhood. Is this what that old Christmas hymn with the lyrics, "Oh tidings of comfort and joy" references? Nope.

But like Zacchaeus, with a familial foundation of faith, my curiosity spiked, and I started to climb. *What if* God is the God of healing?

Pinch me. He did heal all my afflictions. Jesus saw me. Just like Zacchaeus, my little seedling of joy came in the moment.

"When Jesus came to the place, he looked up and said to him, 'Zacchaeus, hurry and come down, for I must stay at your house today.' So he hurried and came down and received him *joyfully*" (vv. 5–6 ESV, emphasis mine).

In another strange sort of way, I relate to the exclusion Zacchaeus faced in his community. Despite being from the line of Abraham, and no doubt a religious man, he was despised by many. That must have stung.

My journey of emotional healing required the process of healing from my history with exclusion. Walking into a room packed full of beautiful, healthy women convinced me that I didn't belong. As I scanned the room, I looked for someone relatable and breathed a sigh of relief when I saw her—knowing I wasn't alone. I now realize this thinking was so bizarre, searching for acceptance in finding other women battling their weight issues.

How messed up is that? In a roomful of a hundred women, I felt so alone and so lost. And I fell victim to the trap of comparison. I carried this guilt and shame for decades.

I hated being "seen" because of my appearance, but I also felt so "unseen." Confused? Yes, I was too. In other words, my soul cried out "look at me," while my shame cried out "please, don't look at me!" I acknowledge my hot mess.

As I followed the nudges in my soul and stepped out in the baby steps of healing, I finally realized Someone did see me. I opened the doors of my heart and invited Him in to get reacquainted.

Don't miss a key part of Zacchaeus's transformation story. Would it be possible for a filthy rich man to join the kingdom of God? Don't forget, just yesterday in chapter 18 Jesus said: "Indeed, it is easier for a camel to go through the eye of a needle than for someone who is rich to enter the kingdom of God" (Luke 18:25).

I dare say Zacchaeus slipped through the eye of a needle. Look at him go and give up everything to the Lord joyfully. Hallelujah!

> But Zacchaeus stood up and said to the Lord, "Look, Lord! Here and now I give half of my possessions to the poor, and if I have cheated anybody out of anything, I will pay back four times the amount." Jesus said to him, "Today salvation has come to this house, because this man, too, is a son of Abraham." (vv. 8–9)

Finally, we land on one of the key verses in the Gospel of Luke. Indeed, these words spoken by Jesus exclaim to the world the purpose for His divinely appointed ministry. We find it tucked into this story of the tiny-statured man, an outcast from society, but one with enough faith and curiosity to ask a big little question, "*What if?*" "For the Son of Man came to seek and to save what was lost" (v. 10).

Zacchaeus was lost, and now he's found. I was lost, and now I'm found. If you are lost, it's time to be found. If you aren't all in, you need a better view. Start climbing your tree. Join us up here in these branches—the view is amazing.

Pondering

What are some of the worldly "tidings of comfort and joy" keeping you from climbing your tree? Health issues, mood issues, financial issues, relationship issues?

How might your life change when you start the climb up your tree? What if Jesus is seeking your wayward or stubborn heart right now? He longs to show you true comfort and joy. Are you in?

Finding Joy

Jesus sees you in your messy life and is waiting for you to look up and receive Him with joy.

Prayer

Heavenly Father, thank You for coming to this earth fully man and yet fully God with the joy-filled purpose of seeking me, a lost sinner. Thank You for finding me and for saving me. Help me to experience the beauty of this message with an everlasting joy. And help me to share this joy with others who desperately need to know about this joy they've been searching for all along. Amen.

The stone the builders rejected has become the cornerstone. This is the LORD's doing; it is marvelous in our eyes. This is the day the LORD has made; let us rejoice today and be glad in it.

Psalm 118:22–24 ESV

THE CORNERSTONE OF JOY

Hello, Facebook memories. I just love them. After my time studying Luke 20, I landed on some emotional memories through pictures of the day I last set foot in my childhood home. Open the flood gates and pass the tissues. I do miss that home and I do miss my parents living less than a mile away.

My parents turned over the keys to the new buyers just days before Christmas, which was less than ideal in our sentimental minds. There would be no "one last Christmas" next to the warmth of the fireplace.

Growing up there, that home had a solid foundation, not only in the brick structure, but in the family foundation too. These are precious memories. To go along with the pictures of my childhood home, God shared some Scripture today with the theme of foundations. I love how He emphasizes His message for us throughout our day.

> But he looked directly at them and said, "What then is this that is written: 'The stone the builders rejected has become the *cornerstone*'?" (v. 17 ESV, emphasis mine).

The memories of home and this Scripture got me thinking about what the Lord laid on my heart for this chapter. It leads me to one word. *Shelter.*

I'm recalling the God of the Old Testament continually wooing His chosen people back into safety, into the shelter of His care. Eventually, those wayward hearts were cast into exile as a consequence of their sin and idolatry. The ancient Israelites continued to reject the protection from their Creator.

Fast forward to this scene in the parable of the tenants in verses 9 through 19. Generations of people had been restored to Israel, and still the chief priests and teachers of the law missed the salvation message in the Scriptures. They questioned Jesus and set out to trap Him with their line of questioning. Jesus knew their schemes and pressed them between a rock and a hard place. He knew they rejected Him and most definitely didn't understand that He is the cornerstone of everything.

Jesus, whom the Law pointed to as the Cornerstone, the Rock, the One on which to stand—the very idea passed way over their heads. Why? Their pride? Their works? Their life of idolatry? All of the above and more will keep them from the shelter of the welcoming arms of Jesus. They knew they were doomed.

I'm weaving my way through this chapter seeking joy and missing it in these verses full of warnings and watchful eyes of those double-dealing with Jesus. How dare they. Don't they understand their entire existence is dependent on a sure foundation?

Back to my story about the home sale—right at Christmastime. After my parent's turned over the keys, they didn't have a place to live. They were homeless. Good thing they had a home on wheels. Their backup plan called for loading up the pickup and hitching up the trailer to head for a winter in Texas. Just days before Christmas. Bah humbug! But they were anxious to reach the warmer climate and reconnect with their snowbird friends. And then a series of unfortunate events threatened to steal the little joy left in our Christmas season. My parent's camper began to fall apart on the expressway, and they ended up stranded in some rinky-dink town near the Kentucky border. The rig desperately needed major repairs before it would travel any further. Not an easy thing to accomplish at Christmastime. So they waited . . . and waited. They were lonely and isolated before isolation was the cool new thing of 2020. My heart hurt for them.

Their camper lacked a sure foundation resulting in big trouble.

Remembering back to my former obsession with purchases of material things to fill me, I recall stopping myself from sinking into despair over the selling of a house. The process of prepping and packing up a home over forty years in the making pricked all our hearts, but I protected my joy from the loss.

I specifically recall God giving me a song in my heart to boost my spirit. The song is by Vertical Worship called "Bound for Glory" and reminds me that this world is not my home. This peppy song leaves my heart rejoicing in the truth that my feet will stand on holy ground and I am bound for glory. Standing on my cornerstone. Sheltered in place.

Speaking of glory, Jesus even gives us a glimpse of heaven in this chapter:

> But those who are considered worthy of taking part in the age to come and in the resurrection from the dead will neither marry nor be given in marriage, and they can no longer die; for they are like the angels. They are God's children, since they are children of the resurrection." (vv. 35–36)

How exciting to picture a heavenly future, included as God's children. Are we worthy?

This chapter reminds us once again, not to live by worldly standards of home. Don't be crushed, smashed, or broken down on this highway of life by rejecting God's plan for salvation.

Instead, cling to God's plan of our heavenly home. The joyful reunion in that home will be our best gift ever. Trust this sure foundation, this cornerstone, and the shelter of His care. It's all part of God's plan. What marvelous joy!

Pondering

This Christmas season, are you feeling far from home, far from a safe shelter? Is there something separating you or causing you to slip off the sure foundation, the cornerstone?

What will you do to stand on the Rock and recover your joy?

Finding Joy

Joy is built on the cornerstone of Jesus's care and shelter for you.

Prayer

Heavenly Father, thank You for the solid ground You provide for me as I journey with You in this world. When I am feeling far from home, please remind me that I am welcome in Your eternal home with You as the Cornerstone. What a day of rejoicing it will be when I finally arrive in my heavenly home. Amen.

Today's Postscript

I hope you will listen to Vertical Worship's song "Bound for Glory."

Shout for joy to the Lord, all the earth, burst into jubilant song
with music.

Psalm 98:4

December 21—Luke 21

JOY TO THE WEARY WORLD

I'm embarrassed to share this, but I need to know if I'm alone in the fears that gripped my heart for decades.

Do you (or did you) obsess about the timing of Christ's return? And not from the fear of being unprepared, but out of fear of missing out on life—your life. I can't be alone in this . . . please tell me I'm not alone.

These worries began consuming my thoughts in my teenage years and continued until He healed my life.

At age sixteen: "Jesus, don't come back yet; I want to graduate from high school and go to college."

At age eighteen: "All right, I'm in college. Keep holding off on that return. Give me time to find a husband. Let me experience marriage."

At age twenty-three: "Hooray, I'm married. I'm so close to the greatest desire of my heart—motherhood. Hold off on that return, okay?"

And so on, and so on. I'm sure you get the picture. Wow, sweet sister, please tell me, do you want a delay? Look what I discovered in Scripture today in Luke 21 making these thoughts seem *not* so crazy: "How dreadful it will be in those days for pregnant women and nursing mothers! There will be great distress in the land and wrath against this people" (v. 23).

Jesus, while warning about the signs at the end of times, makes a point—mothers will find it extra dreadful. If you're a momma bear, like me, this warning cuts straight to the heart. With destruction all around, we carry an extra burden, not only for our safety, but more so for our children. Reading this verse, maybe Jesus understands my attempts to finagle more time on earth. I know He sees our nurturing hearts.

The idea of wars and rumors of wars, earthquakes, famines, persecution, and nations divided sounds altogether frightful. Where is the joy in this chapter?

I think of the state of our world and another song pops into my mind—"Joy to the World." Do you feel more like "Joy to the Weary World" these days?

Do you know the fascinating history of this Christmas carol? According to an article I read on Crossway, Isaac Watts wrote this as a poem to share the message of Psalm 98. "Watts interpreted this Psalm as a celebration of Jesus's role as King of both his church and the whole world."[7] Years later the poem was set to music and provides hope to the weary world.

I hopped right over to Psalm 98 to rediscover a powerful reminder. Not only is this Psalm full of joy, but it also reminds us God is in control of everything. He shares His plans with us. And He forewarns us of His mighty hand of righteous justice.

> The Lord has made his salvation known and revealed his righteousness to the nations. (Psalm 98:2)

> Shout for joy to the Lord, all the earth, burst into jubilant song with music. (Psalm 98:4)

> He will judge the world in righteousness and the peoples with equity. (Psalm 98:9)

Jesus teaches this chapter today for our benefit, not to stir up fear. Sing this Psalm and allow His to joy wash over you in peace. And don't forget He leaves us with a great Comforter in the Holy Spirit.

But we must be cautious about indifference toward Jesus's warnings. Fear will rise up to take us out, so we must equip for battle with the gift of His Spirit of love, power, and self-control (2 Timothy 1:7). Jesus admonishes us not to squander these gifts He gives us:

> "Be careful, or your hearts will be weighed down with carousing, drunkenness and the anxieties of life, and that day will close on you unexpectedly like a trap. For it will come upon all those who live on the face of the whole earth. Be always on the watch, and pray that you may be able to escape all that is about to happen, and that you may be able to stand before the Son of Man." (vv. 34–36)

Wow, my thoughts in my early life seem quite immature when I reflect on the importance of this chapter. I solely watched out for me, myself, and I. My mindset didn't change until I embarked on this joyful journey and Jesus gifted me with endurance. It's the reason I testify to my spiritual healing being the greatest gift of all.

Now I joyfully exclaim, "Come, Lord Jesus, Come! And *do not delay*!" Can I get an amen?

As I gather my thoughts to wrap up this chapter, my pastor delivered another timely message with a story that finishes this chapter poignantly. Place yourself in the scary events of this chapter—as a parent trying to protect your children. Now read this story and commentary.

When Corrie ten Boom was a little girl, her father used to tuck her into bed at night. He talked and prayed with her, then laid his big hand on her little face. Later, when Corrie was imprisoned in a brutal concentration camp, she would ask God to tuck her in and lay His hand on her face. "That would bring me peace, and I would be able to sleep," said Corrie ten Boom.[8]

> One of our Lord's Names is Emmanuel, meaning "God with us." Our dads or moms may no longer be around to tuck us

into bed, but our Emmanuel never leaves us. Sometimes it helps to envision His presence in the car beside us, sitting by us in the pew at church, or leaning over us in bed as if to tuck us in. It's not a matter of visualizing an imaginary person but of recognizing a Friend's presence.

—David Jeremiah[9]

As we count down to Christmas, God is reminding you to intimately embrace the name "Emmanuel, God with us." God with you. God with me. God with our children. And God with our children's children. My pastor added, "All is well." Indeed.

May the truth of His perfect plan bring you peace, comfort, and *joy to your world* at Christmastime.

Pondering

Throughout this chapter, Jesus admonishes us to endure. Do you have thoughts or fears holding you back from trusting Jesus with your future?

Are you squandering the precious resources He's gifted you with? Name a step you will take to face these fears and anxieties over your future and cling to His joy.

Finding Joy

Knowing Emmanuel, God With Us, we can rejoice in His perfect peace, love, and joy to the world.

Prayer

Heavenly Father, thank You for reminding us in Your Word, that despite our worries and fears, You are in control of everything in heaven and earth. Remind me when I am weary to turn to You and worship You with joy for all You've done in my life. Help me to share this joy to the world during this Christmastime. Amen.

And he said to them, "I have eagerly desired to eat this Passover with you before I suffer."

Luke 22:15

December 22 — Luke 22

A CUP OF JOY

Do you watch "The Chosen"? Listen, friend, television viewing is not really my thing, but this series will inspire you and move you to joy-filled tears. I've watched season one three times and anxiously await each new episode.

I love Peter. Simon Peter. He's a relatable character. Peter is portrayed in the show as charismatic, full of energy, a natural leader, and so full of joy and admiration for Jesus.

Yes, I know this is television, but this year I have noticed Peter's responses to Jesus all throughout the Gospel of Luke. Here are a few Scriptures recording Peter's enthusiasm.

> Simon answered, "Master, we've worked hard all night and haven't caught anything. But because you say so, I will let down the nets." (Luke 5:5)

> When Simon Peter saw this, he fell at Jesus's knees and said, "Go away from me, Lord; I am a sinful man!" (Luke 5:8)

> But he replied, "Lord, I am ready to go with you to prison and to death." (Luke 22:33)

Seems like Peter is *all in* with Jesus from the day they meet. He witnesses Jesus's miracles, he agrees to follow Him, he leaves everything behind to work alongside Jesus, and he even proclaims he will go to prison or to death for his Master.

Peter, Peter, guard your heart. In chapter 22, what Jesus warns of next, after Peter's commitment to go to prison and death, is regrettable.

I've always wondered why Peter would do such a thing as to betray Jesus in His hour of need. Jesus knows full well what happens in Peter's heart in this moment. He just warned Him: "Simon, Simon, Satan has asked to sift all of you as wheat. But I have prayed for you, Simon, that your faith may not fail. And when you have turned back, strengthen your brothers" (vv. 31–32).

Next, in verse 33, Peter declares he will go to prison or death for Jesus. Then comes Jesus's prediction of what Peter would really do: "Jesus answered, 'I tell you, Peter, before the rooster crows today, you will deny three times that you know me'" (v. 34).

I bet Peter raised his eyebrows and scratched his head over those words. Or maybe he said, "Yeah, right. Never, Lord!"

Well, we all know Peter did deny Jesus three times, and in that moment the rooster crowed. And Peter turned and wept bitterly (vv. 60–62). This scene broke my heart. I desperately sought joy in between the words. I kept going back over this story, until . . . I found it; I found the joy! In a little phrase I'd glossed over many times. "And when you have *turned back*, strengthen your brothers" (v. 32, emphasis mine).

When have you turned back? When you *return*. Oh, this is so exciting. Do you see the joy?

Our God is the God of "re." He is the God of second chances. That's not all. When He gives us those second chances, He asks us to learn and do something about it. Here he tells Peter to "strengthen your brothers."

Recently, I wrote out my list of "re" words. There are at least fifty words on the list. But these are my favorites: restore, renew, redeem, rescue, revive, reconcile, rebuild, redo, and rekindle. I could go on and on.

We all have the invitation to *return* to serve Jesus. He understands the weakness of man. He knows the enemy is on the prowl with the intent to bring about our spiritual ruin.

But He provides the way out of our wayward turns. He takes our burdens and offers us the cup of His blood—the ultimate sacrifice. He pours out this offering for us with joy.

As I picture Jesus and the disciples reclining at the last supper, my heart skips a beat when Jesus says: "I have eagerly desired to eat this Passover with you before I suffer" (v. 15).

He was eager for this fellowship. Wow, He loved these men with all His heart. This was one last time to rejoice over the friendships in person. It's bittersweet.

At this intimate table, Jesus offered up His body and His blood in a cup. A cup full of joy. I know it deep down in my soul as I develop this relationship with Him. It's a cup that overflows. It's a cup for you and me. And He's always asking us to return to take a seat at this table. Hallelujah!

Back to sorrowful Peter. How did he respond to his blatant denial of His Messiah? We will read the specifics in the final chapters, but I trust Jesus's exhortation to Peter to return and strengthen his brothers.

Jesus woos us back to do the same. When we slip up, He's always right beside us to redirect and realign ourselves with Him.

Don't ignore His guiding hand, His nudging, or His full out discipline. He desires to reignite this relationship.

He will strengthen you for this journey. And if I dare say, He will fill your cup with overflowing joy—you, in turn, will answer the call and strengthen your brothers (and sisters).

May we all, like Peter, enthusiastically go all in. Jump on this adventure. You won't be sorry. I'm over the moon living joy-fueled for Jesus. Aren't you? What an honor to share our stories for His glory. Rejoice!

Pondering

Think of your journey with Jesus. Is there a time when you fully departed from walking with Him? How did Jesus reach you to return?

Make a list of your "re" words and how you might use the significance of these words to point others to Jesus this Christmas. What would be in your cup of joy to share?

Finding Joy

We can find joy in our journey with Jesus, even when we ignore or deny His work in our lives. Jesus is in the business of restoring us to Him with arms open wide.

Prayer

Heavenly Father, first, I apologize for the moments in my day when I deny Your power and love in my life. As I go about the busyness of preparing for Christmas, I may appear enthusiastic about serving You, but I am prone to put worldly priorities above worshipping You. Thank You for being the God of second chances. Amen.

Then he said, "Jesus, remember me when you come into your kingdom." Jesus answered him, "I tell you the truth, today you will be with me in paradise."

Luke 23:42–43

WEEP WITH ME, JOY

Where is Peter in chapter 23? After his denial of Jesus, I bet he's fleeing the scene of the dramatic events taking place in Jerusalem on this day.

It makes sense. Don't we often run away in our guilt and shame?

And other times we flee because we just don't want to be found. Like the times I have a pity party for myself over my circumstances.

Just leave me be to go cry in the corner. While I'm there, my outlook seems hopeless. My joy needs a box of tissue.

This chapter—oh, I knew this chapter would be the hardest part of our joy-seeking journey because here we are at Calvary. From chapter 1, the Gospel of Luke raced forward to the reality of this difficult chapter. Our Savior, Jesus, is nailed to the cross. It is heavy, but we knew it was coming. I've prayed for Jesus to shine the light, to show us a flicker of joy, in this difficult chapter.

All I want to do is weep when I witness our falsely accused, interrogated, ridiculed, mocked, beaten, convicted, sentenced, and crucified Savior bear the brunt of all this unimageable treatment on our behalf. Where is the light in this dark, dark moment in history? Luke recorded the darkness in the supernatural events of the day in verses 44 through 45: "It was now about noon, and darkness came over the whole land until three in the afternoon, for the sun stopped shining. And the curtain of the temple was torn in two."

While Jesus endured the ultimate pain and suffering, do you think He experienced joy? I may have found the moment to emphatically say yes. Jesus illuminated joy no matter the unbearable circumstances.

I found it in relationship. Two men have an equal opportunity to be in relationship with Jesus. One misses the moment, the other wants in for life. I'm talking about the men crucified on the same hill, the same day with Jesus. What do they choose?

"One of the criminals who hung there, hurled insults at him: 'Aren't you the Messiah? Save yourself and us!'" (v. 39).

This criminal appears to be swept up in the frenzy of the gathered crowd. He absolutely has no regard for the fact he is hanging next to an innocent man. He's clueless, concerned only for his own wellbeing—insulting Jesus one moment and then asking Jesus to save him in the next breath.

Surely this man breaks Jesus's heart. He was so close and yet so far from understanding the only way to his salvation.

Well, then the other criminal piped in:

> But the other criminal rebuked him. "Don't you fear God," he said, "since you are under the same sentence? We are punished justly, for we are getting what our deeds deserve. But this man has done nothing wrong." Then he said, "Jesus, remember me when you come into your kingdom." (vv. 40–42)

Don't you just want to stand up and cheer when you witness someone standing up justly and for the sake of righteousness?

Wow, for the first time reading this passage, I see the message of hope through this tiny historical account shared by Luke. I see the process of someone coming to faith in Christ as a true moment of joy, a reason to celebrate. And I'd like to imagine the abundance of joy that washed over Jesus's heart when that criminal saw the light in the darkness of that day.

Not only that, but Jesus wasn't alone on the cross that day. Of course, God held Him tightly, but here I see a man in the same boat with Jesus. Understanding, seeking the relationship. Being relatable. Leaning in for the gift of joy only Jesus gives.

In turn, Jesus comforted this man's heart.

"Jesus answered him, 'Truly I tell you, today you will be with me in paradise'" (v. 43).

Be still, my weepy heart. Jesus, the man of sorrows in this moment, shared the promise for a hopeless man. Talk about a moment of mourning turned to joy.

"Very truly I tell you, you will weep and mourn while the world rejoices. You will grieve, but your grief will *turn to joy*" (John 16:20, emphasis mine).

I've experienced many weepy moments this year during the trifecta of my perfect storms.

My tendency to fear used to send me fleeing. Avoiding life. Pulling the covers over my head.

Again, I relate to Peter. I mean, where is he today anyhow? I sure hope we find him tomorrow because I know Jesus truly loves Peter and longs for him to return to the scene.

I've learned something extremely valuable in this joyful journey with Jesus. It's two simple words, but they are difficult to do all the time—especially in times of sorrow.

Show up.

That's it? Yeah, that's it. How else do you develop a friendship and deeper relationship with Jesus and others? Friend, you have to show up and meet Him in His Word and take Him at His Word. He's the source of truth, joy, and delight.

Even when it means mustering all your courage through the darkness of life. Those experiences, not so delightful! But guess who is showing up for you? Ahh, I know you know these things!

It's plain to me that Jesus will sit and weep with us whenever we suffer. In my own power and control of my past, I would never be this vulnerable. But now I know and understand the emotional process He will bring us through. He gave us feelings for a reason, right?

And after He offers the healing balm of His joy, we can stand up and continue on this joy-seeking path, sharing His contagious joy to the best of our ability wherever we venture.

It's not a Christmas tune, but I have a favorite song I turn to when I need to weep. Listen to "Weep with Me" by Rend Collective and remember that He loves you. Jesus weeps with you. When sorrow overwhelms your heart, press play on this song and know that He cares for your heart.

It's great you showed up today to stand at the foot of the cross. We have to process this to walk out our purpose for Jesus. We know joy will come in the morning—tomorrow morning in our last chapter of the Gospel of Luke. Get ready.

Pondering

Do you have a circumstance in your life making you prone to run and hide from Jesus? Can you find the joy in your grief?

Do you have someone in your life to be vulnerable with? Do you trust Jesus to be this person?

Finding Joy

Even Jesus suffered great sorrow as He willingly went to the cross with joy for us. When we grieve, we remain covered with His joy.

Prayer

Heavenly Father, the events that took place at Calvary fill me with overwhelming grief. Thank You for the perfect example of love and for sharing Your own sorrows in Your Word. Thank you for teaching me today that You will cover my tears with joy. Help me always keep in mind the purpose of the Christmas story, that You came to save me and this hurting world. Let me be a joy-giver today. Amen.

Today's Postscript

I hope you'll listen to the song "Weep with Me" by Rend Collective.

Then they worshiped him and returned to Jerusalem *with great joy*.
And they stayed continually at the temple, praising God.

Luke 24:52–53 (emphasis mine)

BLESSINGS AND GREAT JOY!

Peter, my long lost friend, I'm overjoyed to see you again. I understand you are sad, frightened, worried, and wonder if you still fit in. But you returned. Man, we are here for you. In fact, let's celebrate and shout for joy because our dear friend Peter needs a little cheer.

Truthfully, after the crucifixion scene yesterday, our downcast souls need an extra dose of Christmas cheer. I know, these last few chapters of Luke are actually the story of Calvary that we celebrate on the Easter holiday. I'm trying not to mix them up!

But, indeed, they intertwine. Maybe I'm a slow learner, or maybe Jesus kept me from recognizing the big picture for a reason (He did), like the two men we meet today on the road to Emmaus (v. 16). Praise God, He opened my eyes and ears.

Back to our dejected but not rejected friend Peter. He needs some hope. Look at him over in the corner. Quietly, solemnly contemplating his major mistake. How will he ever make it up to His friend? His friend is gone. He's grasping for anything . . . something to redeem his relationship with the friend he seriously wounded.

In walks a gang of giddy girls with some unbelievable news. The disciples scoffed and laughed at their nonsensical chatter. This scene makes me laugh. You know guys—they just don't get us!

"But they did not believe the women, because their words seemed to them like nonsense" (v. 11).

But Peter, he gets it. In fact, it's the answer to his current problem. As the news startled him, I'm positive he jumped up for joy. Yes, yes! A spark of joy. Certainly, something exciting stirred in his heart because he ran.

"Peter, however, got up and ran to the tomb. Bending over, he saw the strips of linen lying by themselves, and he went away, wondering to himself what had happened" (v. 12).

Now, I don't know about you, but I don't run for any reason. That is one thing I never do. So, this better be good.

Hmm . . . Jesus's linens in the tomb. His body gone. I wonder what Peter pondered in that moment.

Like the men on the road to Emmaus, Jesus is taking His time to reveal the unbelievable story to Peter too. Why would He do this? Why delay the joyful reunions? Jesus speaks to the two men: "He said to them, 'How foolish you are, and how slow to believe all that the prophets have spoken! Did not the Messiah have to suffer these things and then enter his glory?'" (vv. 25–26).

Now I don't believe Jesus is calling them fools in a derogatory manner. No, instead, I believe He is asking this question with kindness and concern. Like, "Hey friend, don't you know? I've been sharing the truth with you for a few years now—how did you miss this?"

These Jewish men know and study the Scriptures, right? But did they do this out of duty to their religion or did they do this from the passion of their hearts? Something blinded them.

It's confusing. But in the moment Jesus showed up, He set the purpose for this momentary blindness. Jesus is about to teach them a lesson with a moral to the story.

"And beginning with Moses and all the prophets, he explained to them what was said in all the Scriptures concerning himself" (v. 27).

Jesus set them up for their moment of belief.

"When he was at the table with them, he took bread, gave thanks, broke it and began to give it to them. Then *their eyes were opened and they recognized him*, and he disappeared from their sight" (vv. 30–31, emphasis mine).

What a remarkable sight. These men went from blindness to being blindsided. What would you do if something like this happened to you? I know what I would do!

Testify.

Let's go. The two men returned to Jerusalem immediately to exclaim the truth of the resurrection of Jesus to His disciples. He's alive; He's alive. It's true!

"Man, we just broke bread with Jesus. You've gotta hear this story." Do you think the other disciples were intrigued? Intrigued, most likely. Convinced? Not quite yet.

"And while they still did not believe it *because of joy* and amazement, he asked them, 'Do you have anything here to eat?'" (v. 41, emphasis mine).

Love, love, love this. Jesus is once again showing us while He is fully God, He's relatable to us as fully man. Give the guy something to eat.

"While they still did not believe it *because of joy*." (v. 41, emphasis mine).

They scarcely believed this moment. Jesus prepared them for years, and yet here they are in the jaw-dropping moment. Unspeakable joy. And I can't help but realize that their doubts were overcome by this abundant joy now spilling from their hearts. Jesus gifted them with this joy during their amazing journey with Him on earth.

My goodness, I wish I could've been there. Don't you? Imagine how far this joy-fueled band of wanderers will travel with this good news.

"You are witnesses of these things. I am going to send you what my Father has promised; but stay in the city until you have been clothed with power from on high" (vv. 48–49).

The disciples received the final earthly blessing from Jesus as their time together in person came to an end. It was such a bittersweet moment.

I don't know about you, but I'm feeling bittersweet about a whole lot of things this Christmas season. The disciples will be missing out on personal fellowship with Jesus while we may be missing out on intimate fellowship with family and friends who are far away or while we are clinging to joy as we struggle with our hardships and weariness.

This Christmas I pray this journey through the Gospel of Luke filled you up and joy-fueled your witness for Christ.

The weary world rejoices. Yes, Lord. We may be weary. But we praise Your name for Your *thrill of hope*.

"Then they worshiped him and returned to Jerusalem *with great joy*. And they stayed continually at the temple, praising God" (vv. 52–53, emphasis mine).

Friend, I've shared with you many words now. I've enjoyed every moment of this journey together. And I couldn't say it any better than those last two verses of chapter 24.

Worship. Always seek joy. And continually stay in the presence of God—most intimately through His Word—every day. Accept His Christmas gift to you.

Good grief, I'm wiping away tears because this is all I've prayed for you—that you may live joy-fueled for Jesus. Go out and share His joy and peace today.

Pondering

Prepare a bit of your testimony from your joy-seeking journey through the Gospel of Luke. Ponder where the Lord has pointed out joy to you where you felt there was none. Think about how the Lord has increased your joy through the Gospel of Luke.

As you gather, what are you prepared to share from your joy-seeking journey from Christmas to Calvary with your family and friends at your Christmas celebrations?

Finding Joy

When we walk with Jesus daily in His Word, our heart is set on continual worship and praise with great joy because of His gift to us from the Christmas manger to the cross on Calvary.

Prayer

Heavenly Father, I worship and praise You for conquering death and being alive for me, Your faithful follower. You have shown me where to find joy through this Gospel of Luke, and I thank You for these lessons. Even in times of weariness and sorrow, I know that Your joy is real and personal. Because You came to this earth to relate to me, I rejoice in this intimate relationship with You every day. Thank You for the *good news of great joy* in Your Word. Amen.

JOY TO YOU! MERRY CHRISTMAS!

What a bittersweet journey we have traveled together, friend. Don't they (whoever *they* are?) say "all good things must come to an end"? Hmm . . . I believe this is just the beginning.

It is the beginning in living out the life Christ calls us to live. We've learned some really practical and powerful lessons from Dr. Luke. And the Word is meant to penetrate our hearts, which brings us to ponderings.

I'm certain God intentionally highlighted this word in Scripture to give us permission to pause, especially during this most sacred season. Indeed, this life is filled with many trials and storms for the entire world.

I don't know about you, but this I believe: Jesus gathers us to remind us of His perfect peace on earth and good will toward men. We needed a break from the weary world, but more importantly, we needed to seek joy. It was never lost but perhaps just misplaced.

This morning I revisited Luke chapter 2 to read the account of the birth of Jesus and the scene with the shepherds. Every single time I get to verse 19, I press pause, and my heart fills with awe and wonder. Can you just imagine the depth of emotion Mary felt in this moment? And in all the moments of Jesus's life? Wow.

"But Mary treasured up all these things and pondered them in her heart" (v. 19).

Just thinking on such things brings tears to my eyes. She probably had plenty of tears, too, as she persevered to protect the significance of a life with Jesus. I can only imagine.

Confession. I've been so weepy the past few days as this journey wound down.

Yesterday I drove down my block and saw a little boy outside alone tossing a football up in the air. He was the passer and receiver. But I witnessed his joy. And that made me burst into tears. Seriously!

Why? First a flood of childhood memories rushed back as I pictured my younger brother doing the same thing as a kid. He loved playing catch by himself. He was that skinny kid full of joy. I miss time with my brothers.

Then I thought, that's all well and good, but that poor kid is alone. I started thinking about the loneliness I've felt this year in my perfect storms of hardships and trials and the fact that our family Christmases are no longer the same without our childhood home. It's just been different, you know? Pass me a tissue.

Do you need some tissue too? Maybe you've endured a lot of storms and changes this year. Maybe it's going to be a different kind of Christmas for you. Are you missing family? Are there empty seats at your table for the first time because a loved one has departed this earth? Or maybe it will be different because of your failing health or financial struggles. Maybe this will just be the most unusual Christmas ever, one of new traditions or scaling back. Where's the hope and joy for you?

One thing we must not overlook in the scene of this first Christmas story is the understated simplicity of one of the most significant moments in God's eternal plan.

Do you think Mary and Joseph felt a little lonely? I sure do. But in the most unusual way, through the birth of a baby, they were never to be lonely again. Their precious child, called Emmanuel, is the fulfillment of God's promise that we are never alone.

This Christmas season, in this Christmas story, you can be comforted in this truth. God is with us. God is with you. And He fills you by the power of His Holy Spirit with peace and joy. Peace and joy—two meaningful greetings in the Christmas season.

There are many times I need to remind myself, "I'm not alone; we are not alone." Music always helps me turn my heart to Jesus, so I pressed play on a newer favorite Christmas song.

If you get a chance, pause and listen to this song: "Emmanuel, You're One of Us" by Rend Collective. Pay particular attention to the bridge of the song.

Now . . . just know you're not alone.

My hope is that you've learned this truth in your journey through Luke. You know He's calling you to surrender, to sacrifice. Your tender heart is intent now to show up.

And maybe this means you need to develop this discipline of seeking joy in His Word every day. Or maybe, if you already practice this discipline, you need to ask yourself, "Is this my delight?" And then maybe, when it becomes your absolute delight, you will become emboldened to declare it to the world! Yeah, that's where this journey leads . . . testify!

You show up. You do the work. You take a deep breath, and you share His joy everywhere you go! Friend, I can testify—this is the not-so-secret formula that transformed my life. If you don't believe me, maybe Paul will convince you in Romans 15:13. "May the God of hope fill you with all joy and peace as you trust in him, so that you may overflow with hope by the power of the Holy Spirit."

That sounds a lot like never being alone. AH-mazing!

Now, I am personally fond of the fruit of the Spirit joy (in case you haven't guessed that yet). But maybe you need love or peace? Or maybe patience, kindness, goodness, faithfulness, gentleness, and self-control. (Oh, that's the tough one!)

These are all freely available to you, but you need to learn about them in His Word before you can apply them in your witness. Trust me, I lacked all of them in my past, and my witness never shouted, "Look at Jesus." Ugh, quite the opposite. Praise God for the beautiful gifts He gives by His Spirit (Galatians 5:22–23). My daily practice in His Word turned into the biggest passion of my life. This gift is free to you too.

I'm confident this journey through Luke filled you with His Spirit. So, with tears in my eyes, I will say goodbye for now. This may be the end of something, but it's just the beginning of everything. Ain't that the gospel truth?

Oh, one last thing. The weary world rejoices . . . now that's a thrill of hope, and it's from my favorite Christmas hymn. If you want to hear the greatest tenor vocalist ever to sing this song, make sure to listen to David Phelps sing "O Holy Night." This classic song inspired our joy-seeking journey together. Enjoy.

Be joy-fueled.

Merry Christmas,

Christine

Seeking Joy Resources

Introduction

- "O Holy Night," recommended performance by David Phelps on YouTube, https://www.youtube.com/watch?v=ElJ0fiD0lkc
- *Countdown to Christmas through the Book of Luke*, blog series by Christine Trimpe, updated December 1, 2020, https://joyfulketo-life.com/countdown-to-christmas-through-the-book-of-luke/
- *Countdown to Christmas through the Gospel of Luke,* blog series by Christine Trimpe, updated December 25, 2020, https://christinetrimpe.com/countdown-to-christmas-through-the-gospel-of-luke/

Chapter 5: Joyful Healing

- Christine's chapter *Finding Freedom from Formidable Food* can be found in *She Writes for Him: Stories of Living Hope* from Redemption Press available on Amazon.

Chapter 7: Joy in Choosing an Alabaster Jar

- "Alabaster," by Rend Collective, https://www.youtube.com/watch?v=zJsLcwScEDA

Chapter 9: "Follow Me" for Joy

- Kaitlin's Bloukrans Bridge jump video, https://christinetrimpe.com/kaitlins-bloukrans-bridge-bungee-jump/

Chapter 20: The Cornerstone of Joy

- "Bound for Glory," by Vertical Worship, https://www.youtube.com/watch?v=qZCqqzqfnNQ

Chapter 21: Joy to the Weary World

- "Joy to the World (You Are My Joy)," by Rend Collective, https://www.youtube.com/watch?v=k7iPgWgeNsk

Chapter 23: Weep with Me, Joy

- "Weep with Me," by Rend Collective, https://www.youtube.com/watch?v=GAGqvq4N_zQ

Chapter 25: Joy to You! Merry Christmas!

- "Emmanuel, You're One of Us," by Rend Collective, https://www.youtube.com/watch?v=uOw0pM1VmXA
- "O Holy Night," recommended performance by David Phelps on YouTube, https://www.youtube.com/watch?v=ElJ0fiD0lkc

Miscellaneous

- Christine's playlist on Spotify, "Seeking Joy by Author Christine Trimpe," Spotify account: christine.trimpe
- "Seeking Joy through the Gospel of Luke: A Christmas to Calvary Advent Countdown," advent calendar from Christine available here: https://christinetrimpe.com/seeking-joy-advent-calendar/
- Learn more about Christine's Health and Wellness Coaching for *Joy-Fueled Living* on ChristineTrimpe.com

About the Author

Christine Trimpe is a former casual Christian who is now passionate about Christ, coffee, and connecting one-on-one with you for some joy-centered conversation. She'd prefer to meet in person, but for all practical purposes, she's eternally grateful for her new and unexpected calling, writing and speaking, in the second half of her life.

Christine's dramatic weight loss success story has been featured in numerous international publications, like *Woman's Day* and *Reader's Digest*. But she'll be the first to tell you that the weight loss was a nice side benefit to the true gift of healing Christ gifted her mind and spirit. She'll have more to share about this weight loss journey and how God flipped the cravings of her soul in her next book (coming in 2022).

Christine's transformation story will inspire you to start or strengthen your own joy-fueled adventure with Jesus. She's been where you've been, where you are, or where you want to be through decades of painful experiences. Whether you need physical, emotional, or spiritual healing, she testifies that as you dig into God's Word, your life will be transformed.

Daily she prays for that one woman, maybe today it's you, to catch the contagious joy that overflows from the words God gives her to share. From examining daily choices through the exciting journey of sanctification, Scripture is full of promises that Christ-honoring health and wellness can be achieved—body, mind, and spirit.

Christine is now a Certified Health and Wellness Coach through the American Association of Christian Counselors and loves the role of being an accountability partner to empower and equip women to make healthy decisions in their lives for Christ. She also writes a lifestyle blog about her low-carb lifestyle and her *Bible & Beans Blog* to share about the unspeakable joy down in her heart. You can find these blogs, details about her coaching services, and all her social media links on her ministry website at ChristineTrimpe.com.

Christine and her husband, Rob, live in her hometown in Metro Detroit with their two cats, Miki and Kitty. They are overjoyed to have their two adult children and one son-in-law living within walking distance. In her spare time you might catch her leading worship in her local community church or taking her grand pup for a walk in the neighborhood.

NOTES

1   "Billy Sunday," accessed April 20, 2021, https://www.inspiringquotes.us/quotes/NLxF_5BDcptSs.

2   "Bible Interlinear Luke 2:19," Bible Hub, accessed March 23, 2021, https://biblehub.com/interlinear/luke/2–19.htm.

3   "How Many Human Generations Are There from Adam Until Today?" Answers in Genesis, accessed March 17, 2021, https://answersingenesis.org/bible-timeline/genealogy/how-many-human-generations-are-there-from-adam-until-today/.

4   "Cultivate," accessed April 7, 2021, https://www.merriam-webster.com/dictionary/cultivate.

5   "Weekly Livestream form Berkley Community Church broadcasted 12/13/2020," accessed December 13, 2020, http://bcchurch.com/main/.

6   George W. Cooke, "Joy in My Heart," copyrighted 1926, accessed April 20, 2021, https://hymnary.org/text/i_have_the_joy_joy_joy_joy_down_in_my_h/.

7   Greg Forster, "A Brief History of Joy to the World," accessed December 20, 2020, https://www.crossway.org/articles/a-brief-history-of-joy-to-the-world/.

8   Corrie ten Boom, *Each New Day: 365 Reflections to Strengthen Your Faith* (Ada, MI: Revell, 2013).

9 "Corrie ten Boom's Immanuel," accessed December 20, 2020, https://www.preaching.com/sermon-illustrations/corrie-ten-booms-immanuel/.

Order Information

REDEMPTION PRESS

To order additional copies of this book, please visit
www.redemption-press.com.
Also available on Amazon.com and BarnesandNoble.com
or by calling toll-free 1-844-2REDEEM.

CPSIA information can be obtained
at www.ICGtesting.com
Printed in the USA
LVHW032057221021
701265LV00003B/12